# FIFTY YEARS
## with the
# GOLDEN RULE

J. C. PENNEY

# FIFTY YEARS
## with the
# GOLDEN RULE

*by*

## J. C. PENNEY

HARPER & BROTHERS, PUBLISHERS
*New York*

*Manufactured in the United States of America By The Haddon Craftsmen, Inc., Scranton, Pa.*

*To*

EARL CORDER SAMS

*My friend and associate from Kemmerer days*

This book is dedicated with respect and gratitude for a life which was a sure sign of that New Life in Christ, which endures.

*Acknowledgment*

For refreshing my memory of events and experiences I must record my indebtedness to *Main Street Merchant* by Norman Beasley (published by Whittlesey House, 1948), and *J. C. Penney: The Man with a Thousand Partners* as told to Robert W. Bruère (published by Harper & Brothers, 1931.)

I wish also to acknowledge the collaboration of Miss Janet Mabie with me on this book.

# FIFTY YEARS

with the

# GOLDEN RULE

# CHAPTER ONE

After supper that day Father and I sat on the back porch in the warm twilight. Summer, 1887.

In the early mornings we drove the two-wheeled cart two and a half miles into the country to our farm. Bluegrass, apple of my father's eye. After the long, hard-working day it felt good to just sit. The air barely moved the leaves of the maples. There was a touch of haze in the atmosphere. Father turned over in his mind the text he would preach on, Sunday, to his Primitive Baptist flock at Log Creek, about twelve miles distant.

Experiences of growing up crowded in on me, some of them going hard and deep. I was twelve years old. Outside of school I had to work hard around the farm. At games I didn't hold my own very well, being undersized. I wasn't often invited with the others to parties. Schoolmates made fun of my clothing, but I had to buy it myself and it was the best I could afford. I felt out of place in the world around me, ill at ease.

I said hopelessly in the dusk to my father, "I don't believe there is any God!"

He did not say anything at all, immediately.

A neighbor's mongrel dog loped across-lots, lolling his

tongue, eying us indifferently as he went by. The maples were motionless against the sky.

I caught a glimpse of Father's expression: a gentling of plain, stern features; some understanding for the feelings of a boy; a touch of sadness and anxiety.

"Jim," he said, with patience, "prisons are full of men who don't believe there's any God."

From the first my parents were an example of goodness to me. They had the hearts and strengths of pioneers—not just in the ordinary ways of Missouri living in the second half of the nineteenth century, but especially in the way their thinking and conduct clung to right as might.

Both of them believed greatly in education. My father was graduated from Pleasant Ridge College near Weston, in Platte County, Missouri, at the age of seventeen. He wrote his oration on "Earth's Benefactors," and in what he included about the lives of Jesus Christ and Martin Luther, among others, his hearers might easily deduce a bent toward preaching the Word of God.

My mother was Kentucky-born. Daughter of well-to-do parents, she lived a sheltered life, even for those days luxurious, with every advantage possible to provide for a young lady of pre-Civil War days. She went to convent school, not because the family was Catholic, which it wasn't, but because the nuns were most expert at teaching young ladies.

Relatives from Missouri took my mother back to their home state for a visit. No one realized that it would be the instrument of changing her life from that of a southern belle to pioneering.

Clouds of civil war began to gather; my grandfather, fearful for his daughter's safety, sent for her to return home at once. In those days a young lady could not possibly travel alone, so it was arranged that one of her cousins should accompany her.

He remained in Kentucky to court Mary Frances Paxton, my mother. He was a son of the Reverend Eli Penney, a hardy Kentucky pioneer who migrated to Missouri. His name was James Cash Penney, and he and Miss Paxton were married.

Several years later, happily sharing a pioneering urge, they went back to Missouri and bought a tract of land from the railroad for a farm home, near Hamilton.

In her southern environment she had never known what it was to do any work, even cook a meal. Now, with rare courage and optimism, she took up her share of the burden willingly, helping my father in a hundred ways to establish their home in that raw, undeveloped country.

Children came in rapid succession; twelve in all, six of them living to adulthood. My mother did the work of not one but three women, loyally, unselfishly, from before daylight to late evening, with patient good cheer, resolute courage, the most unwavering and serene faith in the purposes of Almighty God.

Our farm was almost 400 acres, practically all pasture land. My father carried over from his early heritage a feeling at times almost mystical for bluegrass. A man of spare habits and the instinct to self-denial, his one luxury was this great spread of bluegrass. Though a hard worker he was not a born money-maker. In one corner of the farm there was a small bituminous coal mine, which he leased out on a royalty

basis of five cents a ton. Mainly he maintained his acreage
—not, it is true, without mortgaging—by buying cattle, grazing them, sending them to market. As he couldn't bring himself to touch plowshare to bluegrass, corn for feeding stock
was bought. It made the difference between profit and loss
on his acreage many times, but his solution was to work to
his utmost and rely on the Lord to help his deficiency. We
had little cash money. But there was family feeling among
us, and our necessitous way of living was often a means of
learning important lessons: of self-denial, and thrift, but too
of moral precept, right human relations.

When I was two or three years old my parents, believing
deeply in the value of education and looking ahead to high
school learning at least for their children, put another mortgage on the farm to buy a house near to schools, in the town of
Hamilton. The house too had to have a mortgage on it. All
in all we lived a life of stern yet not distressing economy.

My father's absolute, unquestioning faith in immortality
was constantly before us as we grew up, though perhaps it
was not always easy for us to understand. Such was his confidence in the hereafter that he could sit by the casket of one
of his own children, finding tranquil composure in reading
aloud from Mr. Bryant's "Thanatopsis":

> So live, that when the mighty caravan
> Which halts one night-time in the vale of death,
> Shall strike its white tents for the morning march;
> Thou shalt mount onward to the Eternal Hills,
> Thy foot unwearied, and thy strength renewed,
> Like the strong eagle's, for its upward flight. . . .

My mother's faith was equally strong. She showed it differ-
ently, that's all. A woman of deep simplicity, in the midst of

her work she could often be heard praying, "Lord, have mercy upon me, a sinner!" I didn't understand then what it meant. It filled her children with wonder, who couldn't imagine their mother sinning in any wise; but the thing that stayed with us was her spirit of humbleness, and it will be an example to me to my dying day.

It was in my father's planning for his children that they become self-reliant. Many times I heard him say, "If I had ten boys and a million dollars, I wouldn't give them a dime." He was not a mean man and he was not a cruel one. He simply understood, beyond all question, that self-discipline can make the difference between an effective life and a wasted one. He wanted self-reliance for his children in the way that the long, straight furrow needs a good plowman.

I was eight years old when he felt the time had come to begin my individual grounding in self-reliance. One evening after supper he called me aside and, with no softening of the surprise to me, remarked, "Jim, I just want you to understand. From now on you'll be buying your own clothes."

I suppose the natural reaction of an eight-year-old to such an announcement might be that his parent was making a little joke. Ours was not a gloomy home; still, our jokes were not about money matters.

"But Paw," I said, "my shoes have holes, both of 'em. Could you get me one more new pair, then let me start in?"

"No. You'll have to figure out something. That's the way it'll have to be now."

"Well—all right." Such a situation could hardly be all right in the mind of a boy, or the heart either. But I knew my father's ways. He did not make up his mind in order to change it.

I had no money. In our family children didn't receive allowances; we were expected to do our share of work around home as a matter of duty, with no thought of being paid for it. Though there was no obligation or precedent for paying me for farm work—any more than for getting in stovewood, and other chores—I earned a little from my father, working in the hayfield. I planned to make up the rest of what I would need to pay for shoes by running errands. The people around us didn't do much hiring of errand boys, so it would be slow, and if I succeeded in getting five cents for an errand it would be big pay.

My first pair of self-bought footgear cost $1.00; they were cheap shoes, even for those times—brogans of cowhide, black and clumsy, put together with wooden pegs, fastened over the instep with coarse black enameled buckles, like those on overshoes.

I was disappointed in them, but they were the best I could afford. I felt a little comforted after I took off the ugly buckles and used just the eyelets. It would be pleasant to record that, in a day or two, pride of independence took over, but I cannot recall that it did.

My older brother and older sister sang in the choir of the Hamilton Baptist Church. We went to Sunday school twice each Sunday: in the morning to Baptist Sunday school, in the afternoon to Presbyterian.

My particular companions were the MacDonald boys; their father was a Hamilton merchant. One Sunday afternoon as we were about to set off, Mr. MacDonald looked me over keenly. "Forget to shine your shoes, did you, Jim?" he said, not unkindly. "They don't look very good. Here—let's fix them—" It shamed me, but it was my own fault. The fact was I had shined the fronts of the shoes but not the backs. I took it for granted that no one would notice. The mortification taught me an immediate lesson in thoroughness.

Inasmuch as my buying a pair of shoes wasn't just an incident but the beginning of a permanent responsibility, I had to think how to keep on making money.

When I had the sum of $2.50 and had done some looking around I decided the best investment I could make would be a pig. I could obtain food for it in exchange for carrying away neighbors' swill and cleaning out the pails for them. With the swill I could fatten the pig and sell it at a profit.

Things went quite well. I found a pig for just what I could pay—$2.50—and, although the swill pails were not an agreeable part of the venture, they were a means to an end. The pig rewarded me by thriving, and sold for enough to buy more pigs. Soon I had a dozen shoats.

My father, watching my handling of the business, suggested that it would be all right for me to follow the corn rows after the huskers finished with them. It helped me considerably. I observed that the down rows would give me all the corn I could use. I had dreams of many well fattened pigs, bringing good prices.

Another day came, with an announcement from my father no less staggering to me than the one about buying my clothes.

"Jim," he said, "you're going to have to sell those pigs. I want you to see about it right away."

"But they're not ready yet, Paw—not fattened."

"Well, the neighbors are complaining. One or two pigs—

that's one thing. A lot of pigs—they smell pretty bad, you know. You can't find fault with the neighbors on that."

It was the off season for pork. My shoats were not yet even half-fat. But my father lived by the golden rule in relation to his neighbors, and it was important to him for me to see that I should too.

With a heavy heart I sold the pigs. They brought half what I'd counted on from them. However, it was past and done. I put the $60.00 from the transaction in two banks.

"Two banks?" said my father.

"If one fails, I'll still have enough in the other for clothes."

My father smiled slightly. I had learned something practical about observing the golden rule and made a shrewd decision about money too on my own responsibility; that was good.

In the last quarter of the century series of revival meetings were an eagerly anticipated part of community life, and rural areas were not passed by. During a revival when I was twelve I felt I wanted to join the church.

"Jim," said my father, with concern, "do you think you're old enough, wise enough, to know what you're doing?" He was a zealous man for religion but shied away from emotional expressions.

I thought I understood what joining the church signified and wanted to take the step. Still, his questioning made me hesitate.

The impulse passed. I didn't join the church.

# CHAPTER TWO

I was under the constant necessity of extending my business ventures. The more I grew the harder it went with my clothes.

I had a little money left from the pig incident as, contrary to my expectations, neither of the banks failed.

My father did some business in horses, raising and selling them, and it seemed to me he might help me in that direction. He explained that it would be necessary for me to go it alone though, taking my chances on being worsted in a trade just as he had and making my own decisions and, possibly, mistakes.

"You won't learn by using secondhand experience," he pointed out. "Keep your eyes and ears open; do the best you can."

At the age of twelve I bought a mare, for spritely good looks and because there seemed to be nothing wrong with her. Leading her home I felt well prepared for my father's approbation. But when I put her in the barn she kicked out the side of the stall. "Horse trading isn't learned all in a minute, son," said my father.

I had no real feel for farming, though I did my share of the work willingly enough; it was expected of me, and I had no right to shirk.

Besides reflecting a deep and prayerful urge to serve his fellow-man my father's preaching at the little Log Creek church was part and parcel of the life of the times. Many men worked farms during the week, to free themselves to preach on the Sabbath.

The need for religious ministry was widely felt. Almost no theological seminaries existed as we now know them. There was little professional training or real ordination of preachers. Licensing of "exhorters" prevailed in some sections and denominations. Communions and sects gathered in small groups around such men as possessed sufficient intellect, education, and fervor to lead them in a simple, primitive religious life.

The community tended to regard preachers as a class kindly and with respect—at least up to the point where a preacher might entertain the wrongheaded idea expressed in the Gospel According to St. Luke, that "The labourer is worthy of his hire."

In the more secular direction, county newspapers were wont to print information that such-and-such ferrymen would undertake to "cross all preachers and teachers of christianity who are engaged in ministerial duties (by making the same known) free of charge."[1]

Understanding my father's sincere and conscientious attitude toward his Log Creek flock, and his preaching the gospel as the Primitive Baptist sect interpreted it, at fourteen I was almost unbearably shocked at a climax of events.

It seems hard to believe now, but in those days there was a sharp, concerted antagonism to Sunday schools, stemming

[1]Columbia *Missouri Statesman,* July 7, 1848, and *Missouri Historical Review,* October, 1942.

from public misunderstanding and ignorance of their scope and methods.

Sunday schools came into existence in Missouri as part of missionary efforts from the East to found religious organizations on the frontier. The Missouri Bible Society came into being in St. Louis in 1818. Sunday schools sprang up; soon there was a long waiting list for Bibles.

But there was a bad tension because some people believed in Sunday schools whereas others were suspicious of them. Critics feared "the hoodwinking of children, and attempts to teach doctrines of Trinity, and Atonement." Proponents, on the contrary, looked to Sunday schools to instill spiritual ideals, help inculcate good moral principles, contribute to youthful literary taste, and help children in learning to read. Educational facilities were less than uniform, and it was not unusual for Sunday school to be the only means of education available for the children of an area.

Stubborn resistance was based on the idea that a child should receive teaching from parents, or public schools; conceivably church schools could become a threat to political freedom.[2]

For several decades the controversy regarding Sunday schools raged over wide areas, in varying degrees of intensity.

My father held three particular convictions which brought him in conflict with prejudices of his times. He believed preachers should be educated for their ministry. He believed they should receive stipends. And he advocated Sunday schools.

The fact that his own children attended Sunday school

[2]"Social Reform in Missouri, 1820-1860." Thesis of Marie George Windell, State Historical Society of Missouri.

would have satisfied some men, but my father's social conscience was such that he yearned for all youth to enjoy equal
advantages.

His convictions displeased some members of his Log Creek
flock. A biting controversy blew up, with the result that I
saw my father brought up on charges of holding beliefs
contrary to the best interests of the Log Creek Primitive
Baptist communion. With what seemed to a boy a hasty,
harsh, and wicked disregard for the feelings and service of a
good man, my father was excommunicated.

It did not seem to occur to the people to take action
against my mother or to include her in the process against
her husband. The implication was that she was welcome to
remain. With fierce loyalty and serene confidence in her
husband's wisdom and fidelity to his convictions she rose
immediately to her feet.

"I believe as Jimmy does," she said simply; "you must include me in the excommunication." I think they felt reluctant to do this; it might seem extreme. But she stood her
ground.

The incident filled me with a searing resentment. At
fourteen injustices will rankle. He and my mother had given
so faithfully of themselves, driving the twenty-five miles over
and back in fair weather, my father riding horseback alone
through wind and rain and mud. Week after week, year in
and year out he had been spiritual guide and friend to his
little congregation. Now, in exchange for his devotion, he
was read out of his church.

But again my father turned the incident into an opportunity to point a lesson and a moral to his children. Discerning

that perhaps my resentment was the most agonized, he said to me, "Don't harbor bitterness, Jim. People see things as they see them. It takes time for ideas to take hold."

His thinking, not alone on this but on many matters, was ahead of his time. But the great thing was that he bore himself wholly without bitterness, though his church had been the core of his life.

I wished I could be like him. I believed what he said, marveled at his serene rejection of all resentment. But it was a long time before I could emulate his example. It was twenty years or more before I could bring myself even to set foot in the Log Creek church.

But in after years I had opportunity to relate his attitude to personal problems and thus to profit intimately from council given by a good father to his son.

Three times after severance from his church Father ran for political office. He did not win, but he knew he had made the best fight of which he was capable, and did not waste himself with vain regrets.

The farm was less of a success than we could have wished, and, because Father would not turn so much as a blade of his bluegrass to plant corn, the stock sometimes cost more than they brought at sale. To understand why he accepted this fact it is necessary to sense the intangibles which may enrich a man's makeup.

The bluegrass land—though in one way it was simply a gently rolling stretch of opulent natural grain land—was to him a living carpet of matchless beauty. A weed in the whole expanse was an unbearable blemish, and he carried a jackknife with him constantly, snipping weeds as he found them, to keep this beauty unmarred. To this day I carry that jackknife always in my pocket.

Occasionally he was given a respite from losses, as once when a trainload of cattle fetched a net profit of eight thousand dollars.

But only in the last year of his life did he agree to give over any of the bluegrass land to planting corn. Almost as though the Lord took it into His head to reward James Cash Penney for years of doing without, and the anxiety of never having a real sufficiency, on the 225 acres he consented to turn under a corn crop of 18,000 bushels yielded over eighty bushels to the acre. That year corn went to fifty cents, and, except for a few bushels kept for seed, the crop was all sold at that satisfying figure.

In spite of difficulties Father believed deeply in farming; and in order to give me a chance to understand its opportunities and satisfactions for myself he offered me the use of four acres.

Though I had no real affinity with farming, I considered what crop I could raise to best advantage and decided on watermelons. He knew how to raise them, of course, and I felt I could get him to help me.

Here again I did not fully anticipate his determination to see his children rely on their own efforts.

"Of course you understand you'd have to pay for my knowledge," he said, watching for my reaction.

Such an idea had not entered my head, nor would paying one's father for practical advice seem logical to any boy.

Logical or not, I had no plans for tapping my cash reserve to pay him. So I went ahead as best I could.

With great hard work my acres were planted. Nature favored me. The melon season was good. The vines blossomed, set, filled.

It happened that the watermelons were tempting to the miners when they came from work, hot, thirsty, tired.

When it seemed to me that my crop might be too quickly diminished I put up a tent on a little rise of land, spending the last nights before harvesting there with my dog and a shotgun. Dim figures would move past in the hollow, taking the precaution of holding hands aloft and calling out in the night, "Don't shoot, Jim, it's only me!" I certainly didn't want to shed blood to save my crop, but I would if I had to. Fortunately things did not go that far.

I made some money, borrowing a horse and wagon from my father and peddling the melons; but it was slow, and I felt impatient.

County fair time came on, and it seemed to me I would be able now to realize on all my hard work.

Saturday was the best fair day. I sold some melons around Hamilton in the early morning and then struck off for the fair grounds. I turned my wagon into position, as close as possible to the stream of fair-goers at the entrance.

"Here they are, folks!" I cried. "Get 'em—get 'em—get 'em. Nice sweet watermelons—fine—sound. Take 'em home with you. Ten cents for big. Good ones for half a dime. Get 'em, folks—get 'em right here!"

Trade was beginning to pick up when I noticed my father standing near the wagon, looking at me with stern anger.

"Jim," he said, catching my eye, "pick up and go home. You're disgracing the Penneys."

I didn't know what to make of it. And in front of all these people! But I knew from his face that it was useless to say anything.

I turned the wagon around and drove home, sweating with shame and a feeling of having been treated unjustly. What had I done? Plenty of people sold farm stuff to the fair-goers.

My father came home.

"Son, don't you know what you were doing?" he said.

"No, Paw, I don't." I was hurt, all the way through.

"The folks selling things inside the fair pay for the privilege," he said. "They call the privilege a concession. Concessions come dear."

"But I wasn't inside the fair—I was outside."

"Exactly."

"What do you mean, Paw, 'exactly'?"

"You were getting trade away from others without paying for the privilege on a par with them. That's unfair dealing, son. You should have had the sense to know it."

"I didn't know about the concessions, Paw, paying for them."

"No excuse, Jim. Just like ignorance of the law is no excuse for breaking it. Anyhow, now you know it. Don't ever let me see a son of mine take advantage of others for his own benefit. Think about it, Jim."

I thought about it. For a long time I thought he'd been too hard on me. I had meant no wrong. Even though he said that wasn't any excuse, I thought it should be.

But what he said, what had happened, soaked in. Without my realizing the full extent for a long time, it soaked in so deep that it became ingrained in my way of doing things.

Once again, in his direct, unadorned way, my father had instilled in me a point of honor which, as time went on, revealed itself to me in the form of a foundation stone of human dealing in the business world. Money is important; but the practice of the golden rule in making money—as in every other aspect of human relations—is the most substantial asset of civilized man.

Soon after my watermelon lesson a youth in the town came to me with a plan by which he was sure we would become rich overnight. He was someone I was tempted to envy at times. He had good clothes and lots of them; he could afford various diversions and seemed to me to have a life much more attractive than mine. "What's the plan?" I asked, interested yet wary of anything which could transform one's fortunes rapidly.

"I know where to get my hands on a lot of counterfeit money," he said calmly. "Because of the standing of our families, yours and mine, we can pass the money without anyone suspecting." He looked at me with satisfaction. "Well, what do you say to that, for a plan!"

When I refused to have anything to do with such a wicked undertaking he was disconcerted and I don't think altogether understood the point of view, but he still seemed to think he'd have relatively little trouble in finding someone else to go in on it with him. Nevertheless, he swore me to secrecy.

His proposal worried me so that, for the first and only time in my life that I can recall, I broke my promise and told my father about it. It reassured me to have him say that I was right in breaking the promise.

As time went on, in addition to the watermelon misadventure, other farming experiences only served to convince me that farming was not for me.

I finished high school. For a couple of years, having no more congenial aim in view, I straggled along on the farm. But I was filled with a deep discontent, feeling that I was at a dead end. I had a flair for trading; I was not at all studious, failed to apply myself, and must have been thinking more about making money than getting an education. I had the idea of being a lawyer, though now that seems strange, as I was only the most average of average students. In any case, being a lawyer meant going to college. My father had no money to send me to college. An uncle heard me out but hesitated to make me the modest loan I sought for tuition.

Slowly I was acquiring a pattern of moral and ethical attitudes and values. What I lacked was a means of harnessing them to practical, forward action.

# CHAPTER THREE

Although there had been many mistakes of youth, I believe my handling of the pig and the watermelon matters caused my father to feel that I possessed the makings of a merchant.

There was in Hamilton a merchant for whom Father had a high regard, as a merchant and a man. He would feel content to have me associated with this man, certain that I could learn a great deal from him. The store of J. M. Hale & Brother was unusual for that size community, well stocked and intelligently run.

My father was now ailing. Nevertheless, my future was much on his heart and mind, and, getting up from a sickbed, he went to see Mr. Hale, to sound him out about taking me on as a clerk.

Thus, in effect, he selected my vocation; I was to be a merchant rather than a professional man. Yet he wasn't so much trying to get me a job, in the sense of making the deal for me, as he was pointing me away from something for which he discerned I was unsuited and toward learning fundamentals of something more in my bent, from a man he considered expert, Mr. Hale.

In the opening weeks of 1895 Mr. Hale said frankly, "Well, Mr. Penney, to tell the truth I don't need another hand.

February's always a dull month. But I'd like to accommodate a son of yours. Tell you what I'll do; if the boy wants to learn what he can of the business while he makes himself generally useful, I'll give him $25.00 for the rest of the year, eleven months. It isn't much, and that's a fact! But—well, we'll see—"

The sum of $2.27 a month was certainly modest pay. But I felt strangely contented. I knew that, if I got into something connected with dry goods, I could sell. At last I had found my work in life.

I went to work in Hale's store the morning of February 4, 1895. Nothing could stop me!

Again my clothing, my appearance rose to plague me. The other clerks, all older than I, snickered openly at me; staring at my clothes they gave me a nickname: "Mose."

It confused me. I felt I could sell, knew it was in me to sell; but in this atmosphere of ridicule I couldn't seem to get a start. If I was alert, stepped forward to greet a customer and wait on him, one of the others interrupted, saying more or less openly, "Mr. Hale asked me to take this customer; you might not know yet how to make a sale—"

I knew Mr. Hale to be a merchant's merchant; this is to say, his store was kept to sell goods. Though he would wish me well, he couldn't let business wait for a green clerk to catch up.

Fear took hold of me. I couldn't seem to shake it off. I feared that Mr. Hale would not even keep me on. When I couldn't find in myself the way to cope with the snide tactics of my fellows, I took refuge in other work. I quit trying to sell and began making myself responsible for sweeping floors and sidewalks, sorting, dusting, and keeping stock in neat order. Neatness had been drummed into me at home. And all the time I busied myself with the stock I could get to know it thoroughly, studying it in every detail so I could even close my eyes and tell grade, weight, and price by the feel. I knew I was learning important things. But I was ashamed of my showing at sales. Was my fear shutting off my chance of becoming a merchant in my own right some day?

I ran errands. I made more and more effort to keep the stock in apple-pie order, well brushed, clean, attractively arranged. But I felt myself sliding into the chasm of my fear. I was not really getting anywhere, I told myself. Inside me a voice seemed to say, "You're not making your way here, Jim. At the end of the year Mr. Hale will surely let you go."

In one illuminating flash I vowed that should not happen to me. I would not be confused, intimidated by the jibes of others, prevented by fear from what I had the capacity to do. I can remember the day, the hour, the moment when, clenching my fist, banging it doggedly on a ledge in the rear of the store, I said to myself, "I will not!" I would respect myself and my powers, go ahead and do what I knew I could do, no matter what others did or said.

I believe now that I had what Quaker friends will regard as a leading.

Within some months of following my new viewpoint and resolve, in a sales force of seven I progressed to the point of ranking third. I had a natural enjoyment of waiting on customers and never let one be nipped away from me.

When the first hints of spring were in the air my father felt that his days were drawing to a close. With quiet yearn-ing he took final stock of his children. He knew that his estate would be in debt; what would be the lot of the younger children?

One by one he considered us. "Mittie has her farm," he said; "Elie has his." I was the third oldest living child. "Jim will make it," he said quietly, coming to me; "I like the way he's started out." He smiled compassionately when he came to another brother. "Poor little Herbie," he said. "His legs are just too short." (Time proved him to be unduly apprehensive; "poor little Herbie" became very successful.)

When he died, in March of 1895, he had no money capital to leave me, or for that matter to leave anyone in the family. But he left me an inheritance far greater than money. In that one sentence, "Jim will make it; I like the way he has started out," he left me a spiritual legacy which, time and again, was to lift me consciously out of dark depression to a clearer path of fresh striving and courage.

Our family friends took an interest in coming to me to be waited on in the store. The other clerks gradually ceased their cruel methods of taking customers away from me, and my eagerness to sell was boundless.

I made mistakes, some of them ludicrous.

When I first went to work in the store Mr. Hale, showing me around the stock, said, "Now Jimmy, you'll find some old stock from time to time—it happens in every store. You want to bear in mind something about storekeeping: *profits* are tied up in the last two of the dozen, be it suits, socks, shirts, shoes, what not. Remember this. Remember, too, anybody can sell new stock—the heart of storekeeping—but it takes a real salesman to sell the tail ends of stock."

Well, a young girl came in the store after a pair of corsets.

I got her size—size 19. I went to the shelf and found a pair in that size; I was ashamed that the end of the box had been broken, and stitched, and looked like sin.

Thinking for the moment only of what Mr. Hale had said about its taking a real salesman to move old stock, I showed the corsets to the girl, telling her they were the latest style, even though I knew better.

A saleswoman, busy with a customer across the aisle, excused herself, stepped over and spoke to my customer. "Jimmy doesn't know much about the stock yet; I'll be able to wait on you in just a few moments."

Subsequently I learned that what I had been trying so zealously to sell that young girl was a nursing corset.

The incident taught me a valuable lesson. *Always tell the truth.*

If I were managing a store today and one of my clerks told a lie in order to sell merchandise, I would fire him—or her—on the spot. Not only would it be wrong. It would be poor business.

Occasionally the clerks made sport of my seriousness about the job. After the store had been broken into in the night a couple of times I was given a room upstairs over it and told to keep an eye on things.

One night I was awakened by suspicious noises. Springing to the head of the stairs I called out, "Who's there? I've got a .38. I'm a good shot, so this is fair warning—"

The noises continued. I think now that it was some of the boys in the store, finding out how easily I scared. Anyway, I took a shot down the staircase. Joke or no, that was the end of night prowlers.

When my eleven months, at $25.00, were up with Mr.

Hale, he said voluntarily, "Jim, this year I'm going to pay you $200."

This, coupled with the place I felt I was making for myself by keeping stock spruce, appealing, and free of so much as a speck of dust, gave me a feeling of forward motion. I liked working in a store, would be happy to do it the rest of my life, with the added aspiration—to be in business for myself!

It was rather freely said in Hamilton after Father's death that he left to a wife and six children his blessing, an upright example, and two mortgages: on the stock farm and on the Hamilton homestead.

In an oversimplified way that was true. There was no flaw of ethical sense, no failure to comprehend the meaning of money. Rather it was a result of breaking too little of his farmland to the plow, which, in turn, was a result of something deep, and not meriting criticism, in his nature. And my mother's way of living up to the responsibility left upon her as head of the family indicates the lofty sense of honor and courage which characterized their life together and the counseling of their children.   .

The local banker urged on Mother that the worth of the farm was not equal to the mortgages and advised her to let it go for debt.

"No," she said, with the same firmness with which she had stood up with her husband before the Log Creek folks, "I guess we'll pay our debts off the honorable way." At that moment she couldn't have known how under the sun she would do it. She had never handled even the simplest finances, had no experience of business of any kind. Nevertheless, in the prayerful conviction that the Lord worked unfailingly with those who love Him, she went to work on this formidable undertaking.

She made a garden immediately, to assure simple, nourishing food. She baked extra bread every day, which she sold to neighbors, glad to be freed of the labor of making their own and, into the bargain, to help a woman for whom they had feeling and respect. She sold milk from one of the cows, doing the milking herself.

My older brother and brother-in-law operated the farm now. Mother squirreled away every spare penny, literally, to apply on mortgage payments. It would all take time, but she never allowed herself to doubt that faith with all the creditors would be kept, all debts paid in full.

Toward the close of my $200.00 year, Mr. Hale said with a smile, "Next year it'll be $300.00, Jim." Of the four children still at home I was the only one with regular earnings. I was saving most of my wages.

Between daily hard work and the driving anxiety to get ahead I abused my health, and when the doctor examined me he said, "It isn't very good news I have for you, Jim—"

"But I can't stop—"

"You can do it now, or before long your system will do it for you. You've got to be out in the open air. This isn't the right climate for you either."

"Are you saying—" I could hardly speak the word—"consumption?"

"Not yet. But it wouldn't take much more—"

It was a dreadful blow. If I left home what would become of my mother's determined plans?

"You've got to think of yourself for a bit now, Jim," she

said cheerfully. "The Lord never leaves His children defenseless. You must go west. Have faith. You'll see—"

I hated to leave Mr. Hale too. When I explained to him he said, "Well, Jim, I hate to see you go. I'll reveal to you now—for quite a while I had serious doubts that you'd make it."

The legacy of my father's words flashed across my mind. "*Jim will make it!*" How much of persistence and resolve I owe to his confidence in me! How pleased he would be, that Mr. Hale regretted losing me.

"It's strange," Mr. Hale added. "I can recall just about the day when you changed." He spoke of one or two things he had noticed in particular.

I didn't tell him about standing alone in the rear of the store, banging my fist on the ledge till my knuckles ached, vowing to rid myself of intimidation, domination by others.

I left my savings, $300, for any use my mother found necessary. I took only enough cash to pay my railroad fare to Denver and board until I located work.

Leaving the house I looked back. My mother stood in the window, drying her tears. But she nodded to me, smiling encouragingly.

On the train I thought about what she had said. "The Lord never leaves His children defenseless." It was something entirely in keeping with the feeling and quality of our family life.

As was natural, by this time I had to a considerable extent outgrown my boyish skepticism. Even the bitterness over my father's excommunication had modified itself. As long as I was at home I went to church with great regularity and was much interested in Sunday school. Between those influences and my parents' courageous and high-principled example I was setting out from home rich in spiritual capital.

# CHAPTER FOUR

Riding westward I knew more and more clearly that, for me, it was right to make my way in something other than farming.

I didn't need to be an economist to comprehend that mechanical binders, working in the great Kansas wheat fields, accomplished work done hitherto by a great many human hands. Invention was becoming the servant of agriculture— but the machinery for distribution lagged behind. For lack of profitable markets farmers still burned corn for fuel, or to empty glutted granaries.

In a vague, unformed way mass distribution plucked at my mind, although I had had no occasion thus far to know its working or applications.

But I did have a comprehension of mankind's universal basic needs: shelter, food, clothing. From Mr. Hale I had absorbed the example of studying people's wants as they reflect economic and social standards of the community.

Mr. Hale had the proper contempt of the spiritually honest man for the adage *Caveat emptor*—"Let the buyer beware!" His store exuded the conviction that fair dealing breeds public confidence and good will; that, together, they produce business profits. Constitutionally Mr. Hale was a one-store merchant. He did not envision the store chain as the dis-

tributive member of a mass-production partnership but was
content to concentrate on an effective job in a chosen sphere.

The doctor had cautioned me, "Jim, you mustn't work
in stores any more. You need a dry climate, and to be out in
fresh air."

It was necessary for me to lose no time in getting work. I
was short of ready cash and had to earn regular money.

Pullmans were unknown territory; I rode out from Missouri in the coach, eating the lunches my mother put up for
me.

Sheer arrival at the Denver altitude gave me an instantan-
eous sense of new well-being. Having found in Mr. Hale's
store what I felt keenly was my real niche in life, I decided
to postpone obedience to the doctor's injunction and find
another store job.

As I could tell from people's stares, my advent in Denver
presented a strange sight. Although I left home in June I
had been urged to take my overshoes. Naturally thinking I'd
need my overcoat too, I wore it on alighting from the train,
though it was a bulky garment, striking below the knees.
Fortunately, seeing no snow on the ground, I hadn't put on
the overshoes.

Reading in the expressions of passers-by that such an ap-
parition as I must have escaped from some institution, I
finally took off my overcoat and carried it over my arm.
Weighed down not only with it but with a heavy valise as
well, I made for the business section, looking for a drygoods
store.

I received a liberal education in the diversities of human

nature in the course of my first job-hunting experiences in a strange place. Having brought several letters of recommendation with me I felt that the sensible thing to do was use them.

I presented one at the first drygoods store I came to. Mr. William R. Owen, a cold, austere man, was not impressed. "I haven't any time to read letters!" he exclaimed testily. "Besides, they don't mean a thing. In this store you couldn't steal anything if you wanted to!" I was taken aback at the idea that a letter of recommendation might be the only guarantee that I wouldn't steal, and didn't think I would want to work in that store anyhow.

A few more stores needed no hands, or discounted the value of references too, or offered too little pay. I expected and was willing to do more than a dollar's worth of work for a dollar's pay, but still, circumstances did make it necessary that I earn a certain number of dollars, cash pay.

The Joslin Dry Goods Company offered $6.00 a week. I took the job and found a place to room and board for $4.50 a week. With enough clothing on hand to last awhile, and a margin of $1.50 a week, I could forget myself in learning my job in a new place.

There were soon problems in getting my share of business in competition with clerks who looked on me as a greenhorn at selling, and a "foreigner" from Missouri as well.

One morning a customer asked me to show eider down. Just as she said, "I will take—" the clerk who was senior in point of time with the store, and my most aggressive competitor, stepped in, saying, "I will wait on the lady now."

When the sale was made, the customer gone, I said to him, "I want to tell you now—if ever you do that to me again, I will thrash you." It was pretty belligerent and there was the practical factor that he was bigger than I. He walked away snickering but, except for some incidental sniping, stopped interfering with my sales.

I felt that I had made an open stand for fair play and, when I found another job and quit to take it, that I could leave a moral victory behind me. Although I had been rigorously inculcated with the golden rule by Father, he had wisely prepared my mind to accept the fact that the millennium has not arrived and that, until it does, all men will not bind themselves to observe it.

Familiarizing myself with the stock of a store down in Larimer Street where I was now working, I noticed that certain items, among them men's socks, were for sale at two prices. To me this was such a wrong idea that I took it for granted there was an error in marking. Surely no merchant would deliberately use such methods, for he would realize the importance of fair dealing with customers.

I took the socks to the proprietor. "There seems to be a mistake here, sir," I said. "Which price is the correct one?"

He studied me narrowly.

"As you see," I pointed out, "one mark is twenty-five cents a pair, the other is two pairs for a quarter."

"Young man," he said sharply, "kindly mind your own business. You're here to sell things, not mark them. Do as the price marks say. Sell the socks for twenty-five cents a pair if you can. If you can't, sell them two pairs for a quarter."

"But sir—that's—that's not—well, fair—"

"Sell the socks!" he shouted. "Don't spend your time teaching me!"

Back at Hale's I hadn't been taught to do business that way, nor would my parents approve of it. There was no use in my continuing to work in a store that supported such a policy. I asked for my wages, got them, and left.

What should I do now? I needed more experience. I needed to earn more money. Denver seemed too big, not the place for me. I had the feeling for small towns, understood the people. And I had a dream, though it seemed far off, of being in business for myself.

I saw the notice of a shop for sale in the town of Longmont, about forty miles north of Denver. A butcher shop. Having grown up on a stock farm it struck me that I could buy the stock—which would keep me outdoors, as the doctor had urged—and hire a man to look after the butchering.

I wrote my mother, telling her that it seemed the chance to go into business for myself and asking whether she could spare my savings of $300.00 so that I could take advantage of the opportunity. Without a word of doubt she sent the money.

I hurried to Longmont and bought the shop. The bold lettering of my name on the window served my vanity; a bull's head was painted over it, and *Meat Market* underneath. It may just be that there was something prophetic in my selection of the bull's head for the venture.

According to the butcher, who had had previous experience of that particular location, my success would depend heavily on the trade from the hotel. "To keep the hotel for a customer," he explained, "all you have to do is buy the chef a bottle of whisky a week."

At first I didn't give it much thought. I simply bought the whisky and gave it to the man. But I began remembering how my father, deeply aware of havoc wrought in human lives by strong drink, had impressed the danger on the minds of his sons. Then it struck me forcibly that if he were alive he would be sadly disappointed, seeing me use whisky as a bribe for business gain. I made up my mind to buy the chef no more whisky, and never again to pursue profit in such a manner.

I explained to the chef; but the butcher had not exaggerated and I lost the trade of the hotel. Since it bulked so large in success or failure for the butcher shop, I lost that too and at the age of twenty-three I was flat broke. In my heart I knew it was right never to let go of a principle to hang onto a job. I did not regret taking the stand, but it was a costly lesson.

I had noticed in Longmont a dry goods and clothing store which somehow reminded me strongly of Hale's, back in Hamilton. It was owned by a Mr. T. M. Callahan, and I went to ask him for a job.

He looked at me closely. "Aren't you the butcher-shop young man?" he inquired, showing that my fame had preceded me!

"If you give me a job, Mr. Callahan," I said boldly, "I'll show you whether or not I can sell goods. Give me just enough to keep body and soul together. I can prove myself to you."

I wasn't interested so much in the wages I could get, or bothered by long hours; I was looking for opportunity. I knew that Johnson & Callahan had six stores or more; if I could get on as an extra clerk, with a chance to become a regular, I could make good. If I didn't, I would know that I was to blame, no one else.

He rubbed his chin thoughtfully. "Well, I've got all the permanent help I need at present. Still, one of the clerks is out sick—want to come in for the holidays while he's away?"

"Yes, sir, I do." I thought I could make such a good showing that, even when the other clerk came back, he wouldn't want to let me go.

To be happy I needed to be behind a counter again. I was out to sell goods. It was like being home after journeying into a far country; it was good, being back, selling good goods to people I understood.

All in all, my employment with Mr. Callahan cast a long, long shadow. From the first day, in addition to being as hardworking a salesclerk as I knew how, I made the job teach me about all sides of the drygoods business, as fast as I could learn. There were some incidental differences between Callahan's and Hale's, and I learned from them too. Mr. Callahan was perhaps less inclined than Mr. Hale to keep strict tabs on both clerks and stock. This I noticed in connection with a rather curious and irresponsible foible on the part of a salesclerk.

A pile of suits, all one pattern but in a fairly good range of sizes, remained unsold for months. At first I was puzzled. Finally I asked the clerk who mainly sold men's suits why he thought the stock failed to move. Calmly he explained that he liked the pattern and had bought one of the suits himself. As he wasn't anxious to meet himself on the street, so to speak, he simply pushed suits of other patterns than his own.

Mr. Callahan was evidently unaware of this surprising maneuver.

Mr. Newcomb, the manager of Joslin's store, invited me to go to church with him and his wife a number of times. Somewhere comfortably in a storeroom of my being was my backlog of spiritual capital, and the church and Sunday school experiences of my growing years. I went with the Newcombs but it was rather perfunctory for I hardly thought of anything in my waking hours but getting ahead in storekeeping.

In the store I worked at selling like a Trojan, not only because it was what I was there to do, but because there was an excitement about it to me—"new every morning, and fresh every evening"—in developing the ability to move stock.

For a while after the holidays I was kept to work on inventory. But soon that was done, and soon too the clerk who had been sick returned—you might say to my job. As I expected Mr. Callahan to speak about it anyway, I brought up the matter myself, asking if I should look for another job.

"Not if you'd be interested in working for my partner and me in another town," he remarked.

I could hardly control my elation over the very idea.

"My partner, Guy Johnson, and I have a store over in Wyoming: Evanston. He worked for me first here in Longmont; then I got him to go and open up a new store in Evanston. He didn't go there as my employee but as my partner, with a share in ownership of the store. We think there's worth in the idea of a partnership chain."

A partnership chain! I had never heard before of even a

chain of stores. Young and inexperienced as I was, all sorts of possibilities for such an idea seemed to stream across my mind.

"Well, what do you think?" said Mr. Callahan. "Johnson needs a man."

On the twenty-ninth day of March, 1899, a year and nine months after leaving Hale's store, I presented myself to Guy Johnson in Evanston, and he hired me as junior salesman, at $50.00 a month, twice what I would have received if I had been able to stay with Mr. Hale through my third year. The opportunity of my lifetime was now firmly in my grasp!

Although I had seen enough to know it was something of a display custom in those days, I was a little taken aback at first by the appearance of the store. A great deal of stock hung in festoons from the ceiling and it seemed to give a pretty cluttered appearance. But I caught myself. "Who are you, to criticize a successful merchant!" I said inwardly and set about interesting myself in more important matters.

I concentrated on two points: knowing the stock and exactly where everything was, and giving the customer the utmost in service and value.

I was particularly interested in the idea of keeping the store sold out of old stock. It meant something more to me than merely the cash tied up in odds and ends of slow-moving merchandise. It was the belief that good merchandise need never stay unsold; moreover, there is no excuse for a store to contain anything but good merchandise. To me it would be a sign of something out of kilter that the shelves of a store were never quite cleared of shopworn tail ends. Besides, I had learned the lesson well that the profit on the dozen lot rests in selling the last two.

Mr. Johnson took note of my flair for neatness, and kindred detail. I remember that once he noticed another clerk packing a box in slipshod fashion and decided to give us an object-lesson. He first had the clerk unpack the box on the counter (so he wouldn't get any idea that I had tattled) and then had me repack it. Together we studied the wrong way and the right to pack a box.

Many years later, as an interesting aftermath of this incident, I had a letter from the same clerk. He recalled the matter, commented on the fact that my name was over more than a thousand stores. "Why did it happen to you instead of me?" he wrote. "Is it because you were smarter, or luckier, or what?"

All the time in those days with Johnson & Callahan I thought about getting into business eventually for myself. I must! Yet how on earth would I ever save enough—even if, literally, I could save every penny I was earning, which was of course impossible—to set myself up independently?

I have often been credited with originating the drygoods chain store. The fact is that Callahan and Johnson both had the basic idea before me. In itself the chain has an ancient and interesting history. Mitsui in Japan goes back to 1643; Fuggers, of Augsburg, to the fourteenth century; in America the Hudson's Bay Company and the Great Atlantic & Pacific Tea Company, to the first transcontinental railroad; and so on.

My experience as an employee of both Callahan and Johnson did give me an insight into broad possibilities of such a method although, at the time, I was limited by lack of practical experience to only the faintest inkling of what it could mean to storekeeping as a vocation and to public buying.

I had another, personal, reason for wanting to get into business for myself. While working in Longmont for Mr. Callahan I had met a young lady whom I wished to marry. I could marry on $50.00 a month if I could be assured of earning more in a reasonable time.

Meanwhile I gave my whole mind to working well for Mr. Johnson. Early in my employment the head clerk invited me to eat lunch with him. As soon as we finished I got up.

"Where are you going?" said my associate, looking at me with some curiosity, for he was going to sit in the park for a while with his cigar and the newspaper.

"Back to work."

"Don't be foolish. Don't you know there's an hour off for lunch?"

But my mind kept running over things at the store which needed to be done, and I couldn't see the sense in just sitting around waiting for clock hands to move a given distance.

It got to be a saying of the head clerk's, "Well, Penney never knows when it's time to quit." The point was that by finishing up whatever I was doing, I often delayed his getting out, because he had the keys and the responsibility of locking up. What he said was really a kind of compliment, though I did not take it to be meant as such.

I wrote to Miss Berta Hess in Longmont, asking her to name the day. On August 24, 1899, with $100.00 I had saved and a mileage book borrowed in order to make the trip, I met her in Cheyenne and we were married.

We set up housekeeping in a tiny house, and my wife brought her church letter from Longmont and put it into the Evanston Methodist Church.

From the moment I married, I had a real helpmeet. Many a night when she sensed that I wanted to keep on working at the store she packed my supper in a tin pail and brought it to me. Very often she supplied me with hints about how to add service and value from the woman's point of view, and I felt that, whatever position of independence I might grow to in the future, in my wife I had my first and invaluable partner.

One day when I had been working a little less than a year in Evanston for Callahan & Johnson, the mayor of Evanston offered me a job at $100.00 a month, to open a store for him in a near-by town. Turning the proposal over in my mind I saw that such a store would be bound to take away some of Mr. Johnson's country trade. Besides, Mr. Johnson was away, so I told the mayor I would have to wait to talk over any such change with him first.

Mr. Johnson was in the East, buying merchandise. When he got back I told him about the offer. He put no barrier in my way, but talked to me long and seriously about the plans he and Mr. Callahan had for branching out and, when they did, the need they would have for the right men to open and manage new stores.

He didn't offer a thing that was specific, but somehow I was settled in my mind that the people I wanted to be with were Callahan and Johnson.

A little later Mr. Johnson said that in the spring they were going to open a new store. "We've decided we want you to take charge of it," he said. "And we'll arrange for you to buy an interest, as a partner."

The opportunity I had dreamed of!

Hitherto these two men had operated only in small towns. Across the Wyoming border lay the Great Salt Lake, in Utah; between Evanston and Salt Lake City was the promising city of Ogden. Already it had a population of 35,000. It was on the main line of the Union Pacific. The golden spike had been driven in '69 but the boom spirit that had hovered around the construction gangs was still strong in the region.

Mr. Johnson's mind was set on a store in Ogden. On a Saturday, when it would appear at its busiest, he and I went down to look it over.

It was a flourishing place, all right; no question about that. Mr. Johnson was as excited as a boy on circus day, but he was careful to let me form my own impression.

Finally, after hours of walking, and not a word from me, his curiosity got the better of him. "Well, what do you think? Why don't you say something?"

For me, innately, cities were places to keep away from. Small towns were where I was at home. I knew how to get close to the lives of small town people, learning their needs and preferences and serving them accordingly.

"Mr. Johnson," I said, knowing he was going to be disappointed, "I don't want to come here. This place—well, it's too big."

"Too big? How could a place be too big to do business in? But, say for the moment that it is; where do you want to go?"

"Well—Diamondville. Yes, I'd like to go to Diamondville." I'd never been there. But in Evanston I'd waited on Diamondville folks. I knew their kind. They were my kind.

It was a disappointment to Mr. Johnson. He was genuinely convinced that I was wrong. However, we went back to

Evanston and soon he and Mr. Callahan went over to inspect the Diamondville region.

Mr. Callahan did not think Diamondville was the place. "Kemmerer is the place for you," he said. He and Mr. Johnson told me to go over and look at Kemmerer for myself. But it would cost me ten or fifteen dollars, and I was willing to accept their judgment.

Then, suddenly, Mr. Callahan changed his mind. A friend of his described how his three sons had tried a store in Kemmerer and it had failed. "They were as bright as young Penney. Don't send him there," he advised Mr. Callahan.

But the more the hazards were listed, the more determined I grew to prove that I could run a successful store in Kemmerer. Having made up my own mind, I began questioning every customer from Kemmerer who came to the Evanston store. What kind of goods would the miners and ranchers favor? Could they give me names of friends who would trade in a good store in Kemmerer?

And I went to see the town. I looked in on the hardware store. A busy hardware store in a community means the kind of people I understand and like: home-builders, the kind of folks who take pride in things of good quality, take pride in their way of living. I went into the bank, and the blacksmith shop, for the same reason.

The cashier of the bank thought I would be making a mistake and explained why. The men in the mining camps got paid only once a month; the company issued trading coupons —which the saloons were quite willing to accept!—A cash-and-carry business would have competition in a situation like that, and so forth. . .and so forth. . . .

"Mr. Pfeiffer," I said, "I believe you will be surprised at the cash-and-carry business we'll do. We are going to open a golden-rule store in Kemmerer."

Mr. Callahan and Mr. Johnson were still uneasy. They didn't want me to have the set back of a failure and sought my wife's influence with me.

"If Jim wants to go to Kemmerer—or, for that matter, to the top of the Wasatch Mountains—" she said, "then I'm going with him."

She and I had been able to save only $500.00, although my salary had been raised from $50.00 to $90.00 a month. The store would open with a capital of $6000.00; I would have a one-third partnership for $2000.00. Mr. Callahan and Mr. Johnson were prepared to lend me the needed $1500.00, at the going rate of 8 per cent.

Mrs. Penney and I talked it over. We decided to seek the money in Hamilton first. There were two banks there. I wrote to one. If they turned me down there, I would find out why before going to the other.

The Hamilton bank agreed to lend me $1500.00 at 6 per cent.

When I told Mr. Johnson he smiled. "You went to all that bother, when you could have got it from us? Why?"

"I saved 2 per cent. I saved $30.00, and all it cost me was a postage stamp."

Where business is conducted on a large scale, the difference between failure and success is often a difference of only 2 per cent.

# CHAPTER FIVE

When the sun rose over Kemmerer, Wyoming, April 14, 1902, it gilded a sign reading

*Golden Rule Store*

and I was in business as a full partner. The firm name was Johnson, Callahan and Penney, but it was used only for book-keeping purposes.

There were many golden-rule stores, doing many types of business throughout the West. But the name was a poignant link for me with my father's and mother's ideals and injunctions. For me it had the creative meaning of one of the most fundamental laws that can be expressed in words. We speak of it as having come down to us from the Sermon on the Mount. Of its real origin little is known. We find it specifically stated in the literature of eleven religions. While Christ was not the first to give it expression, His was the perfect pronouncement.

For hundreds of years after the golden rule was spoken by the Master, men were prone to regard it more as a beautiful formula for idealism than as a law which would work practically if utilized in the everyday life of men and women. In the narrow scope of relationships between neighbors and friends it could perhaps be practiced with some success, people said, but it was not regarded hopefully for universal adoption.

As civilization grew and horizons widened, the definition of "brotherhood" took on more exact meaning, and people came gradually to understand the golden rule as a basic principle, applicable to all relationships.

In former periods business was identified as *secular,* and service as *sacred.* In proportion as we have discerned that between secular and sacred no arbitrary line exists, public awareness has grown that the golden rule was meant for business as much as for other human relationships.

Hence, in setting up a business under the name and meaning of the golden rule, I was publicly binding myself, in my business relations, to a principle which had been a real and intimate part of my family upbringing. To me the sign on the store was much more than a trade name.

It is easy to be wise after the fact. In the light of later experience I wish it could be recorded that we had a moment of prayer before we opened the door for business, asking God's guidance and blessing for the venture which was all-important to us. The fact was we were thinking that morning only of business. We had assumed a big responsibility, and our minds were taken up with all the labor of beginning to do business in a place where failure had overtaken others before us.

Fliers and handbills which I had distributed far and wide did a good job for me. It is human nature to want to save on purchases. Even the cash prices on the handbills couldn't keep away the miners. Also cash-and-carry held an appeal of honest value to the people of distant farms and ranches.

When we locked the store at midnight and went upstairs
to our attic room after the first day's business to figure out
how we stood, there wasn't a great deal of paper money or,
for that matter, so many silver dollars; but there was an
astonishing—to us—wealth in pennies, nickels, dimes, quarters, and half-dollars. Our first day's sales amounted actually
to only $33.41 shy of the $500 savings we had put with the
note for $1500 to pay for the partnership.

We felt chary of counting too many chickens on the
strength of one day's experience. But there seemed no great
harm in telling ourselves that some of the predictions about
Kemmerer as a business location might have been unduly
pessimistic. I remarked to my wife, with a certain relish,
"What do you suppose Mr. Pfeiffer in the Kemmerer bank
is going to say to this?"

Having made the point of a new store by opening up at
sunrise on the first day, we then settled on an opening of
7 A.M. Closing time was when no more people in the streets
seemed to be heading for the store. Saturday nights that
meant at least midnight.

We couldn't make perpetual-motion machines of ourselves
and on Sunday opened the store at eight o'clock.

For a long time there was no thought of attending church.
We accepted Sundays as a particularly busy time in the store.
On Sunday sheep ranchers could take the time to drive into
town. Miners, who worked six days a week, had time to enjoy
leisurely shopping.

Nudged in the conscience of my Baptist upbringing for
working on the seventh day, I soothed it with the authority
of Jesus' rejoinder to the Pharisees, "Wherefore it is lawful

to do well on the sabbath." I am afraid the fact is that, while I did set high standards for dealing with the public, my mind in those days was solely on doing business, Sundays as well as all the other days.

We were soon so busy that we had to hire help. The mining company maintained three camps. Whereas the company stores treated their customers rather callously, in our store the people were quick to notice a different atmosphere, which made them feel welcome and appreciated. They realized that we sold goods at just one price, and gave good service along with our fair prices. Many of the miners were foreigners; when their countrymen arrived to take jobs in the mines their first experience in town was being brought into the Golden Rule Store by their friends, our customers, to be fitted out with work clothes. The turnover in employment was high. I got the reputation of being hard on help. I was. You can't keep store with one hand tied behind you. But I was as hard on myself, never asking more of any employee than of myself. I had a big responsibility to my partners for the confidence they had reposed in me. To get ahead, to roll up profits in which we were all to share, I had to build up the business as rapidly as I knew how.

The more work I did, the more we all did, the more there was to do. In this compounding of work lay the prospects for success. Each day must count visibly. When summer came on, farmers and ranchers wouldn't be able to use their horses to drive into town. The miners would work only two or three days a week then too.

If I had that part of it to do over again; if I were starting out again in a raw environment only waiting for development, I believe I would drive as hard as I did then. In the face of such a challenge there is justified ruthlessness, akin to the ruthlessness of Nature at the moment when a new life is born.

After the first novelty of the Golden Rule and its appeal to Kemmerer wore off, it was not unusual to hear it said in the streets that J. C. Penney was money mad, even "a fool." It is true we made money; we were there to build the business to healthy strength. It is also true that we took our slogan "Golden Rule Store" with strict literalness. Our idea was to make money and build business through serving the community with fair dealing and honest value. The necessities of the community dictated our action. I like to remember that, if a few employees did not continue with us, because they found J. C. Penney too hard to work for or were not in sympathy with our goal, many others who were at Kemmerer with us then stayed to grow up as associates with the J. C. Penney Company.

A case in point is Earl Corder Sams. Coming in with me as a clerk at Kemmerer, he succeeded me as President of the J. C. Penney Company and in time became chairman of the Board.

Before we had any help, however, my wife and I worked from early morning to late night, putting every ounce of our energy and creative enthusiasm into the store.

Often after we had locked up and gone to the quiet of the upstairs we sat by the potbellied stove and reviewed things. The matter of my growing reputation in the community for being money mad, for instance.

"Some day I'm going to have a chain of drygoods stores

that will cover these mountain states!" I said thoughtfully. "As I see it, money is properly a by-product of building men as partners. The men I hire will have to fit the right pattern if they are to qualify for partnership with me, just as I had to qualify with Johnson and Callahan. They'll have to be sincerely anxious to learn, and not only willing but eager to work. Success is first of all a matter of the spirit. When I see a young man or young woman identifying him- or herself closely with the work to be done, so closely that the closing hour can pass unnoticed, then I recognize the beginnings of success. If I seem 'money mad' as they call it, I'm not interested in the money for itself, but as a means to hire men who, carefully selected and trained, capable of assuming responsibility, will then become part of this whole partner-ownership dream, realized in a chain of drygoods stores covering these mountain states. In reality it will be a chain of men held together by an idea."

The kind of folks who lived in and around Kemmerer made all the difference.

Born of the Oregon Short Line railroad and the bituminous coal mines, the town stood at the gate of the Inland Empire. The mines produced a good grade of long-burning, high-flame coal, and the Golden Rule Store and an inrush of miners arrived at about the same moment, in 1902. Trains, coming in along the route of Lewis and Clark, stopped to take on coal before going on over the Wasatch Mountains and down into the Inland Empire. Short branch lines ran into the hills behind Kemmerer, connecting with two stage lines, running north and east. The back country offered good land for grazing, and prosperous sheepmen would come into Kemmerer to buy. One third of the 12,000-odd people in Lincoln County were children in school. They were people who took the saving of so much as a penny seriously. To save pennies for them I had to save them for myself. We threw away no wrapping paper, no short ends of string, no empty boxes, no nails, even though they were bent, for they could be straightened and used again. I had been trained on my father's farm not to waste a seed potato or an ear of corn or a squash seed. Why should I waste string in the Kemmerer store, or nails, or even a piece of wrapping paper?

To open another store my partners had sent out from Longmont a man who had been with them a long time. He became dissatisfied with his location at Rock Springs—he had not been given an interest in the store—when he learned that I was at Kemmerer and had a one-third interest in the store.

"Penney's the luckiest man I ever saw!" he complained.

"It's not luck," Mr. Johnson commented. "It's pluck."

The store at Rock Springs not coming along as it should, my partners offered me an interest in it on the strength of my Kemmerer showing; they thought that, if I gave him a hand, he might perk up.

He was a hard nut to crack! As it happened, I found out, he had joined a band. When they were hired to play for an entertainment or dance, he was quick to close up the store for the sake of the $5.00 he would get for playing.

It was nothing against him as a man, but a good deal against him as a merchant. For a while we struggled along, but when it became clear that storekeeping just didn't fit his nature, we ended the situation. I selected another man, and the store became a success.

In the course of that time also I had opened up another store as third partner, at Cumberland. No need to borrow money this time, as my share could be bought with Kemmerer earnings.

As Cumberland was a mining town too, the coal company which controlled the mine kept a store of its own. First off, therefore, our store had to locate outside town limits, as per instructions from the coal company. It occurred to me that they thought this would change my decision to open a store.

We located as close to the town line as possible, and the store went well right away.

It was good for me in more ways than just cash receipts. Three stores were much more responsibility than I had imagined shouldering at that stage of my experience as a merchant. I could no longer set the pace of the partnership idea as I chose. Along with managing, I had to select and train men, and more, and more, men.

I never hired anyone who did not have a positive belief in a Supreme Being. Creeds were not discussed, and I made no great point at that time of a church connection either. But I would never have an atheist in a store of mine.

Mrs. Penney and I made do with the packing-box furniture we had started out with, the empty shoe boxes for chairs. There was a well-nigh perpetual mud puddle in front of our store, which was flanked on one side by a cheap boarding-house and on the other by the Chinese laundry. When our first baby was born, the crib was a crate padded with old clothes.

But our confidence, the busy hours, were more strength and comfort than upholstered furniture and solid silver could have been. My wife worked in the store side by side with me as much of the time as she could, wrapping the baby in a blanket and putting him down for naps under the counter while she waited on customers. At the end of the first year alone we had done about $29,000 worth of business, at an overhead which was almost laughably low.

I attributed our progress considerably to our understanding of people who worked with their hands: farmers, laborers, and their families. They were the kind of people who grasped what we were doing and, because we dealt squarely with them, gave us their trade.

Having to keep my hand on not one but three stores, I was away from home a good deal, and, although my partners and I wrote back and forth constantly about store business, meetings between us were infrequent. So I had no idea it was in their minds to dissolve their own partnership, and that therefore they would want to sell their interest in the Kemmerer, Rock Springs, and Cumberland stores.

But in late 1907 this was their decision and they came to me, offering me their interests in the three stores for $30,000.00.

"I'd like the stores," I said. "I can't give you a lien on any stock in the stores as security, because it would affect my credit. But I will give you my personal note for one year, at 8 per cent."

"All right," they said. And so the papers were signed.

Twelve years from beginning to learn from Mr. Hale how to be a merchant, I was now J. C. Penney, merchant, in business for himself.

With two children in the family we outgrew living in the

attic of the Kemmerer store. I bought a small house across the road. My wife did the housework and looked after the children, naturally; but three times a day she crossed over to the store to give me time to go home and eat meals. There was an unfinished half-story to the house, and she finished that, covering it with building paper. She decided, too, that a shed in the rear of the house would be useful, and built it herself, of wood reclaimed from drygoods boxes.

The pattern of partnership which I was now carrying on as my own made it necessary to hire men who could be expected to do much more than just work for an employer whose sole interest lay in making money. I myself was willing and able to do anything in the store that needed doing, and, even if it were sweeping the floor or sidewalk, the men I hired had to be willing and able to do so too, if the need arose.

I like to remember that all through my business life I've swept store sidewalks whenever I noticed that they needed it, and I still do it. I suppose sweeping sidewalks would seem a rather insignificant job to some, not likely to be any important part of experience. But I am not so sure of that. Recently I was reminded by E. M. Christenson, now in the Personnel Department of the J. C. Penney Company, of an incident which occurred back in Washington State.

In 1916 Mr. Christenson was working for the Company at Moscow, Idaho, on an extra basis while going to school. I recall now that, at the time, I was on the way to Portland on a stock train, going to attend a show. The train was made up of cars for prize cattle and horses, with one passenger coach for those of us who liked to go along with their stock. The train stopped over to feed and water the stock, so I took advantage of the opportunity to go up the street to visit our store for a few moments.

This is the way Mr. Christenson recalls the incident:

"During the summer vacation period I was sent to help out in a near-by store, Colfax, Washington. I was only a youngster sixteen years of age, and naturally knew very little about the merchandising business, or any other field of endeavor.

"We opened the store at 7:30 A.M., in those days, and I was always most anxious to arrive every morning before the manager, a Mr. White.

"One of my first duties in the morning was to sweep the sidewalk in front of the store. One morning, while hurrying to work, about 7:15 A.M., I noticed from quite a distance that someone was sweeping off the sidewalk—doing my job!

"I managed to get into the store without being noticed by the party who was doing the sweeping, greeted Mr. White, who was waiting on a customer, and quickly grabbed a dust-cloth and turkey-tail duster, proceeding to give the stock on the men's side its regular morning dusting.

"Mr. White soon finished waiting on his customer and came up to me, saying, 'Earl, did you meet our visitor?'

"I said no, that I had only noticed him sweeping off the sidewalk.

"'Well, you know who he is, don't you?' said Mr. White.

"I shook my head. But before I could say a word the stranger, still holding the broom, was standing beside me. Mr. White said,

"'Earl, I want you to meet Mr. Penney,' He went on, saying some things about me and my job, but I was so excited and confused that I hardly realized what I was doing or hearing.

"Here was the man I had heard so much about, founder of the biggest company I had ever known of, the Golden Rule Stores, standing right there and shaking hands with me, a sixteen-year-old kid who was frequently even embarrassed at approaching customers.

"But I recovered sufficiently to hear Mr. Penney say, in a kindly way, 'Young man, what is your ambition?'

"I told him I wanted to be successful like he was, and that I was willing to work hard to learn.

"For a few minutes he talked to me, leaving these thoughts with me:

"1. Clean habits and Christian principles, coupled with hard work, will work wonders.

"2. The golden rule will work for you if you will apply it diligently.

"3. A spirit of true service to the customer is necessary.

"4. Selling is our No. 1 job. Never get away from selling a lot of merchandise personally. The more you sell the more you learn.

"Mr. Penney impressed these thoughts upon me so indelibly that, if I tried, I couldn't forget them, even today.

"Incidentally, I returned to Colfax to manage that store seven years later, in 1923. There is no doubt in my mind but what Mr. Penney's inspirational talk to me, standing there with my broom in his hand, played an important part in helping me to progress with the J. C. Penney Company."

In Kemmerer sidewalks were an aggravation to us. Our store on Pine Street was beyond the triangle. The triangle—a variant of village square—held the Kemmerer business section. Befitting that fact, there were cement sidewalks around the triangle and a continuous hitching post. But off the triangle, where we were, the wooden sidewalks still stood. They were of soft wood, rough, really impossible to spruce up no matter how often they were swept. However, we did not bow to that fact to get out of sweeping them!

I never have spied on men, I studied them. Did a clerk come back from lunch before the clock told him to? I noticed, to discover if it reflected an industrious habit of mind, and ambition. Was the floor "clean enough to eat your dinner from"? There I would undoubtedly find a man determined to succeed, and to work to do so. Did a clerk's sales mount consistently? Make a note of him for a future partnership!

After things took shape all around, we kept the Kemmerer store open only a half-day on Sunday. But that half was still the morning. Farmers and people from the ranches did their trading on the way to and from church. Our own children were still too young even for Sunday school, and we concentrated our attention on making money, and the golden rule a reality.

All too heavily, I came in later years to see, I was living without question on the spiritual capital with which my parents and home influences had endowed me.

I was frankly taking it for granted that it was enough for a man to lead a moral and upright life. Practising the golden rule in my business benefitted everyone who came in contact with me. Surely that was being a practical Christian!

I had to pass through many years, many clashes with life, before recognizing that what seemed to me sufficient was much less than what Christ taught.

# CHAPTER SIX

My confidence that business progress and a literal interpretation of the golden rule could be worked out together went straight back to my father's example.

From the time I was a young boy I had understood, that though he worked at two separate callings, by his *way* of working at them he made them interchangeable. He was a farmer and he was a preacher, and to him there was no real difference in what these two occupations demanded of a man. He plowed, planted, harvested—and then, when he preached his sermons, applied his industry with the same quality of feeling so that, in effect, he had one over-all ministry: to serve.

I was, now, selecting and training men to work along my lines of storekeeping, permeating our dealings with the public with the specific spirit of the golden rule. To be the servant of people who were my neighbors and my friends; to prosper as a by-product of serving and enriching them—it was a problem, and a fascinating challenge.

At about this time my efforts to find just the right person to carry forward this whole idea brought me in touch with the man with whom I was to travel the years of almost a half-century. Curiously enough, it was mainly my golden rule emphasis that caused him to hesitate over connecting himself with my plans.

Like myself, Earl Sams was a farmer's son, with a predilection for storekeeping rather than farming land. Yet, though looking for a position with larger opportunities than the one he had at the time, in Simpson, Kansas, Sams felt the Golden Rule to be a suspiciously common trade name, hence "it makes you think twice about taking a job with any man who uses it!" Perhaps I may say without indelicacy that, happily, we were not together long before he was convinced that its meaning and use were literal with me.

Some of Mr. Sams' friends back in Kansas were not sure he was doing the right thing. When he gave thirty days' notice as manager of the Simpson store, the owner said, "You won't like it. But I'll keep your job here open, and you can come back."

When Mr. Sams came to Kemmerer for the first interview with me, and to look around, he paid a visit to the cashier at the First National Bank. It was this cashier who had entertained grave doubts that a cash-and-carry store could compete with the company coupon system.

"Tell me honestly, Mr. Pfeiffer," said Mr. Sams, "what do you think about J. C. Penney?"

"He's scrupulously honest—and he's also a hard man to work for," Mr. Pfeiffer told him plainly. "You'll work long hours, seven days a week, and he'll expect an awful lot of you. But I can tell you too—it won't be more than he expects of himself. That answer your questions, young man?"

"How do you think I'll get along with him?" Mr. Sams wanted all the information about me that he could get, but that was all right, no more than I wanted about him.

I was looking for a man anxious to work and make rapid

advancement. He wanted a place where he could do what he knew how to do, and be sure it would get him ahead.

Mr. Pfeiffer said, "I'll answer that this way. If you're the type of man Penney's looking for, there's another merchant in Kemmerer you might like to talk to."

"How's that?"

"Well, some other proposition might be as good, if not better, for you."

Mr. Sams took the advice and went to see the man. He was offered a store managership at what turned out to be $25.00 more a month than I would pay. He said he'd decide after he'd talked with me.

He didn't tell me about the other offer. Instead, he questioned me about one point in my preliminary letter to him.

"Mr. Penney, you said I could have 'plenty of rope' if I came with you. What, exactly, do you mean by that?"

"It means that you can climb as fast as you like. The faster you climb the better it'll suit us. This is simply a chance for you—or anyone else—to make good, if you're competent. Willingness is an exceptional quality."

When he first looked us over at Kemmerer, Mr. Sams noted that our stock was clean, well kept, though the general appearance of the store, to his way of thinking, was rather junky. Nevertheless, he decided that he liked the spirit and the principle by which we operated. So, in October, 1907, he came to work with me, for that reason and because he was a man, like myself, who liked storekeeping.

I saw in one working day that he was a good man behind a counter. People liked him. He made friends easily and, equally important, kept the friends he made. And he was interested in working. The first Sunday after he arrived in Kemmerer he was at the store on the stroke of seven o'clock, ready to get to work. We'd forgotten to tell him that Sunday opening time was eight o'clock; we hadn't yet given him a store key.

History repeated itself when the others joshed him for his eagerness, exactly as I'd been joshed in Evanston. It didn't bother him. The point was, he was up and ready at seven; he was as determined to succeed as I was, and for the same reasons.

Before the winter was over I knew he was what I'd hoped, believed, he would be, when I hired him.

To protect the sinews of a growing partnership plan in which men, and the confidence of men in one another, and their loyalty to all and to the underlying idea, meant the difference between growth and mere existence, I made a rule to place men in tryout stores first, to prove their capacity to carry responsibility alone and show the manager-quality of character and preparation. After that came partnership, with one-third ownership interest.

I believed thoroughly in the plan of Callahan and Johnson, whereby clerks were trained to become partners in new stores. But I also believed it was a mistake to put partnership ahead of positive evidence as to the stable capabilities of men for partnership. A partnership represented two-way opportunity;—for the grantor and for the recipient. No good could result from moving people before they were equal to responsibility.

The decision to try out Mr. Sams as manager meant giving him the Cumberland store, which was as tough a situation as we had. The store was a mile from the center of town and bucked the inherent and psychological opposition of the company store. The place was cramped, about 25 x 40 feet, with two rooms at the rear for the Samses' home. Without modern improvements, they had to lug water about a half-mile from the creek. The water was muddy most of the time and had to settle, in a barrel, before it could be drunk.

Some years later Mr. Sams remarked to a convention of managers, "We went there to begin business and make our home, and never thought of it as a sacrifice. We understood that the business was in process of making. We were just proud to be a part of it, without any definite promises, or intimation about the length of time it would take to do our share in working out the future. Many times since, Mrs. Sams had said our year in Cumberland was one of the happiest we've ever had."

It is only honest to say that, all through those years, our minds were exclusively taken up with business and making money. We were building on a foundation which was morally strong, and ethical.

Those were days when it was widely accepted that a man could not create a fortune and, at the same time, be a Christian. I wanted very much to disprove the idea, and to do both. I believed it was possible. The mistake I made at that time was confusing the moral and ethical code with a Christian life which was dynamic. Speaking for myself, I didn't spare the right amount of time and thinking specifically for God, along in those years. But I now believe God was working a guiding, restraining influence on my life long before I perceived it, or became aware of my responsibilities in relation to it. It seems to me that, though I do not excuse them, my neglect of those years did create an even richer opportunity and experience in later days, when hard events were the instrument of showing me where my faults had lain.

Take the neglect of prayer, for instance. It is absurd to pray on rising and consider that that takes care of one's relationship to God for the day. Actually the challenge of living effectively makes it necessary to pray all through the day. How wisely has it been suggested, "Very brief thoughts, private mental invocations, can hold a man firmly in the presence of God. Then truly all conduct is inspired by prayer."

This does not undervalue the set time for prayer. Rather it widens the door to functional relationship with God. Perhaps my sensitiveness to this in later years has been the keener because in the earlier years of my independent business life I lived too prodigally on my spiritual capital, took too much for granted as to a relationship with God.

The facets of giving value and good service, as I myself would wish to be given them, were endless.

While still actively heading the Kemmerer store I went to St. Louis on a buying trip, an aspect of storekeeping in which Mr. Johnson had given me my first grounding. The buying of one item chanced to bring out rather an important point in relation to dealing by the golden rule.

I needed to buy children's cotton stockings. Two top grades presented no discernible difference, either in feel or in look. But there was a difference in price of ten cents per dozen pairs. I bought at the higher price of the two.

"Now, you're an experienced merchant," I was reminded. "If neither your fingers nor your eyes detect any difference, why didn't you buy at the lower price and save the ten cents?"

"How, then," I replied, "could I tell customers I was offering the best stockings I could buy?"

"The customer would have no way of knowing the difference."

"I would know," I said. "The fact that I knew would be the difference. When I say merchandise is the best, it must be the best. That's plain business integrity. In my stores we aim not to dilute that prime element, integrity."

At the end of the year Mr. Sams went to manage the Cumberland store. I invited him to become a partner in a store in Eureka, Utah. More and more it was clear to me that what I envisioned as a business was a just economic environment, underwritten by a moral rather than a money bond. The laws running it would be written in the character and on the hearts of the men I selected and trained for partnership. Men of character never break moral bonds.

I shaped my plan. When a store manager had enough money out of store earnings to finance a one-third interest in a new store he was allowed to do so, providing he had trained a man to manage it for him.

In this way our personal trainees would become our partners, and, sending the head man in one store out to manage a new store, we would be dividing the two principal people in each store into equal halves, with the result that each half became an entity in itself and, simultaneously, the nucleus of further stores.

I explained to Earl Sams that, if he thought well of the

plan and wanted to come in with me on it, he or I or both could put up the two-thirds money needed to start the new stores in which he and I would be interested. In my adaptation of the partnership idea to which I had been guided by my former partners, Callahan and Johnson, Mr. Sams could continue to get all the rope he could use.

In 1909 things were moving in a way which seemed to warrant a new phase. I gave up managing the Kemmerer store personally, and moved Mrs. Penney and the boys to Salt Lake City.

It was in my mind that efficiency and economy would be increased by setting up one central buying office, with an experienced man to do the buying for all the stores. In this way more savings could be passed on to our customers.

My partners didn't take to the idea. In their management they made a point of knowing their customers, were convinced that no outsider could understand the differing characteristic customer needs, and were determined to continue their own buying for their own stores. Although at variance with my view this attitude showed an independence which was healthy.

The borrowing of money to acquire my one-third interest in Kemmerer had shown me the importance of bank credits. Now and then I borrowed from local banks in small amounts, but they were not geared to finance large-scale operations. Salt Lake City brought me into the orbit of larger banks and was a good vantage for visiting existing stores and studying location potentials for new ones.

Our two boys were nearing the age when they should be

going to Sunday school. Mrs. Penney and I sought out a church of her denomination, and the boys began going before long to the Sunday school of the First Methodist Church.

The pastor was the Reverend Francis Burgette Short, a forceful speaker and a man of striking appearance and personality, standing six foot four.

It wasn't my habit to carry much cash on me. Finding only a dollar or so in my pocket the first Sunday we attended the church, I put a check in the collection.

Later Dr. Short explained that he put the check in his pocket for the purpose of making a note of it. While he was sitting at dinner he got to thinking that anyone who put a check in the plate must be a stranger in the congregation. He thought he would find out who I was and pay a pastoral call on me, which he soon did, and our family became regular attendants of his church. It was the start of a friendship which was to develop into an interesting and versatile association of Dr. Short with the Penney Company, and a strong support to me personally in later crises.

Church attendance was pleasant and I enjoyed Dr. Short's sermons, but I must admit that, at the time, it was all rather a passive gesture of all-round living. In a vague way I told myself that a man's duty was to support the church with money in addition to living in a conscientious and upright manner, but that it was not particularly necessary to go further. My mind was immersed in business plans, the daily-growing possibilities for the partnership idea. When I thought about it at all, I told myself defensively that I wasn't a good enough man anyhow to be a church member. There was considerable public discussion about the hypocrisy often found in the churches, the insincerity of using the church affiliation for one's own ends. If I just attended church naturally, and gave what I could to support religious work, I would probably compare favorably with most men in meeting the responsibility.

Dr. Short naturally differed with me in this view, talked frequently with me about it. But business demanded so much of my attention and time that I was in no hurry to take more positive action.

I was more and more captivated with the potential power of the partnership-manager idea to hold men together. I myself had the sound experience of being one of three partners, in Johnson, Callahan and Penney. I had a financial interest in every store that started out of Kemmerer, Cumberland, Eureka, Bingham Canyon, and other locations, under men I had trained and for whom I supplied two-thirds of the initial capital. Then each of the new managers was helped in turn to launch a new store, provided that the store of which he had charge had accumulated sufficient capital to start the next store out of earnings; provided also that he was able to find and train a new man capable of taking charge and, in due course, developing a new link.

All this pioneered away from the human assumption that no hardheaded businessman, having made a financial success, would dream of letting properties of proved value get out of his complete control, into the control of others. It took the far sounder view, on the contrary, that in a business such as ours the premier asset was, not money, not buildings, not land, but *men*—men inspired by confidence in one another, who could envision their success in a framework of the success of their business associates, not working *for* one another, but *with* one another, in the sure and certain knowledge that their sins and good deeds alike would be visited upon every other man with whom, in the unique pattern of chain organization, they were linked.

In terms of business it was indeed an example in miniature of the principle so memorably expressed by John Donne: "No man is an Iland, intire of it selfe; . . . any mans death diminishes me, because I am involved in Mankinde; And therefore never send to know for whom the bell tolls. . . ." Our formula, rooted in a creative everyday practice of the golden rule by each individual in the organization, was in the firm tradition of Christian living. *Respect yourself; respect others; work hard and continuously at some worthwhile thing* was our motto. Growth was the proof of its practicality.

By 1910 our chain and the branching system of chain-partnerships were in full swing. Thanks to my family environment and the training received from Mr. Hale and my partners Callahan and Johnson, I knew how to get at the hearts and needs of our kind of people, how to run a store of our type. I knew how to select locations in more towns now, where people were ready to welcome the kind of service we were prepared to give. I had learned how to select men of the right type for the stores, men of character, enthusiasm, and energy. My wife was an active help in this. In 1908 we had had four stores, with gross sales of over $218,000.00; in 1910, fourteen stores, grossing more than $660,000.00.

We were all small-town and country boys, many of us having made fumbling starts in other work, catching fire now with an idea for which we were suited. It wasn't our way to invade small towns and villages out of the blue, as Norman Beasley put it in his *Main Street Merchant* like snake-oil peddlers, to make a quick cleanup, then disappear again into thin air, leaving people with empty pockets and nothing of value to show for their money. We were settling permanently, as small-town men born and bred, who understood our neighbors as readily as they could understand us. And in coming among them to stay, it was with an idea beneficial to all.

As time went on, among those who joined with me at least twenty-five men had been boyhood friends in and around my home town, Hamilton, Missouri. These included the five MacDonald boys, whose father had given me the timely lesson in shining the backs as well as the fronts of my shoes. After incorporation of the company two MacDonalds became directors, one continuing seventeen years, the other J. M. MacDonald, twenty-six years.

As the whole structure gained the permanence of stability, the thought crossed the minds of Mrs. Penney and myself that, eight years after buckling down in Kemmerer, we might with reason allow ourselves to take a belated wedding trip. We decided on Europe.

The doctor advised my wife to have her tonsils out if she were going on a sea voyage. It was necessary for me to make a last-minute business trip. I wished the operation postponed until I got back, but our trunks were packed, and Mrs. Penney felt that she could get the nuisance of the hospital errand out of the way while I was absent.

She was so inured to saving every penny possible to help

my business that she wouldn't take a conveyance to our home when she left the hospital, although there was a very severe rainstorm. She caught a heavy cold, which rapidly ran into pneumonia.

I was barely able to reach home before she died, December 26, 1910. In that hour my world crashed about me.

To build a business, to make a success in the eyes of men, to accumulate money—what was the purpose of life? What had money meant for my wife?

I felt mocked by life, even by God Himself.

# CHAPTER SEVEN

I didn't pray during this chattering experince, for the reason that I could not. The plain fact is, I had not learned how to pray.

Loneliness and fear sometimes drive a person in desperation to prayer. But for many years now my course had been so rooted in reliance on myself, my own powers, that there was no latent impulse toward any outside source of strength.

It took time, and searing experience, to even admit into my mind the idea that, blessed and enriched as I had been by the attributes of women such as my mother and my wife, I should find it possible to temper grief with humble thanks to God for the priceless companionships of the years. But the earth had slipped from under my feet, and insupportable loss held my mind.

The two boys were pitifully young to be left motherless. There was a merciful responsibility for me in the readjustment needed for them and their future.

We continued to attend the church. Dr. Short, the pastor, came to me and discussed whether I would care to establish a memorial to my wife in the form of paying off the mortgage on the edifice. This was in line with several talks we had had on the subject of using one's money for philanthropic and related good purposes, and I felt grateful to him for suggesting a practical memorial which I could feel would be in keeping with my wife's desires. When the time came, Dr. Short's boys and my two joined in a simple event marking the burning of the mortgage.

So far as the business went, it was expanding dynamically. Our pioneering type of operation toned with the pioneering temper and condition of the mass of people in that part of the country. Whereas people may have been inclined at first to suspect that our somewhat unique stores had seized on using the golden rule for purely commercial advantage, they changed in proportion as their firsthand knowledge told them that they were better off for our being among them. Their money went farther because of our cash-and-carry rule. They felt at ease, at home, in our stores. We never had, or pretended to have, "sales" misleadingly offering "$1.50 value for 98¢" and our customers understood why. We sold absolutes in value for absolutes in fairness of price. Thus people were led to trust us, to value our service, to trade with us because they learned for themselves that we took the golden rule literally.

I believed then, as I believe today and shall to the end of my days, that when a man truly works with a principle, such as the golden rule, that principle makes him the representative of a great and positive working force. Then a creative force of the universe is back of him, for the principle is doing the work, while he merely attends to the details.

Yet at this time for me personally, with my wife gone, some necessary part of the zest too seemed gone. I was badly dissatisfied, restless. I debated prolonged travel, the relief of getting away from everything. Common sense told me, though, that it could be only a false relief; the only hope of running away from things is to prepare to run endlessly. Even then, will they ever really be outdistanced?

Many decisions about the business competed for my attention. The boys, by now, were settled in boarding school.

Up to this point in my life I had never been troubled by any interest whatever in drinking and liquor. My father's attitude on the subject had permeated my growing up, and I just never had thought of it except as an evil mistakenly succumbed to by others.

Now, however, with an insistence as inexplicable to me as it was strong, I felt driven to find in drink a way out of despair and grief. Intuitively everything in my nature was against it. I couldn't even account for the presence of the tormenting urge.

Night after night, for weeks passing into months I walked long hours alone, blindly battling the ceaseless assault on my will and nerves. I grasped at business trips to New York to escape surroundings filled with memories which had become painful. When the day's business was over I walked through the dark, deserted corridors of the impersonal city, along the tangled streets of the lower East Side until I came to the river. Often I stood on some lonely coal dock thinking, as I watched the silent waters, how much better off I would be if I were just to go quietly under them.

On my first trip to New York after my wife's death I left the Broadway Central Hotel one evening with the idea of walking until exhaustion should overtake me, giving me some hope of sleep.

It was winter. After a while I found myself wandering along the Bowery, which runs along under the Third Avenue El, and presently in Chinatown, with its atmosphere of mystery.

As I walked wearily along I began to hear fragments of sound from the rescue mission. Through a crack in a loosely hung door the strains of an old, familiar hymn, "Jesus, lover of my soul," sifted out into the dark chill of the night.

Out of bone-tiredness, and the nagging of the wind, and some curiosity, I stepped inside the mission, slipping into a seat at the back of the room.

A man was telling a story of rescue from a drunkard's life, and his countenance made an immediate, profound impression on me. He was dressed sprucely in the height of fashion; it was hard to visualize what he was saying—that through drink he had sunk as low as it is possible for a man to go.

He had lost his job, lost his friends, been deserted by his family. At last, disgraced, a bitter caricature of the man he once had been, penniless, sick, he had literally been picked out of the gutter by folks from this rescue mission and cared for until he could get on his feet again. Now he was in charge of the rug department of a big department store.

"I found Jesus Christ in this place," he said simply, his face alight. "I never had known Him before. It is surprising —no matter how low we sink; how we forget the precious things that were taught us by saintly mothers and God-fearing fathers; how badly we have repaid Him in the past for His loving-kindness and tender mercies, He will always welcome us back to our home in His family. His patience with us is endless, his mercy eternal.

"If I can express to you men in my lame words the joy that is in my heart tonight, the debt I owe to Jesus Christ and, through Him, to the good people of this rescue mission—"

There was a message for me in that man's words. Sitting there quietly (at the time I thought by such a thin margin of chance, but later I wondered if it had been chance at all) somehow I knew it.

In my distraught state I did not altogether grasp it clearly. But I felt that my steps had been led in some way that night, halfway across the city, along the murky Bowery, through Chinatown and into Doyers Street, to Tom Noonan's Rescue Mission.

As usual I was carrying little cash. However, without disclosing personal burdens or making myself known to anyone, I left a check with one of the staff. It began a habit, the least return I could make for what I sensed was a blessing of far-reaching significance in my disrupted life.

In the stores, volume sales were increasingly large. Whatever my inner turmoil, the business futures of many men were involved with mine. It was imperative that I make a sufficient peace with life to go on with the idea which bound us together.

The condition for growth of the idea was quality for low price. Packing the customers' dollars with value required rapid turnover of goods, with a small profit on each sale. This posed large problems of capacity to take advantage of discounts for cash, close buying at wholesale, buying in line with known local demand, accurate knowledge of customers' wants, and so forth.

From the outset new stores had been financed as a rule directly out of immediate earnings of existing stores. Yet I have found it wise always to look on rules as guides, rather than as shackles. My own one-third interest in Kemmerer had been bought by money which in large part was borrowed. It had conveyed an important lesson to me in the value of bank credits.

As the business grew and prospered, problems of expansion indicated increasingly that the volume of personal credit was going to be insufficient. We had proved our philosophy—that the right and best way to make money is as a by-product of making men; that men are effectively made by the responsibility they carry as manager-partners. We came to a point at which, after sound legal advice, the managers themselves proposed that they should entrust to me, as surety for whatever credits I deemed necessary from the banks, all that they owned in the stores. Which, for most of them, was all they owned in the world.

Next to the words of my father—"Jim will make it; I like the way he's started out"—this was an unsought vote of confidence which I shall prize most, to the end of my life. In legal parlance it was a subrogation agreement. To me it was a tremendously moving testament of faith.

In some measure, therefore, I absorbed myself again in the Golden Rule Stores, attacking involved problems with a certain reviving sense of pioneering adventure.

In this period, as each new manager was helped to launch a new store, with capital deriving from the store he was in charge of, the store would be owned by him together with Mr. Sams as well as others. When such a store was prepared to link another store into the chain, calling for a fourth man to take charge of it, I would drop out. Thus, over a period of time, there came to be stores in which I personally had no legal share of direct ownership. Groups of men could have broken away if they had felt like it. But they had thoroughly caught the underlying spirit of the partnership idea, and did not.

During 1911 and 1912 twenty stores were added, bringing the number of our type of Golden Rule Stores to thirty-four, in eight western states, including Oregon and Washington.

Another of our early men, Wilk Hyer, was looking for opportunity ahead of big money. Missouri born and bred, he had been in business for himself with a small store at Springfield in the Ozarks. He closed out the store to go farther west, seeking greater opportunity.

I met him and engaged him as first man for our St. Anthony, Idaho, store, which opened in the spring of 1910. Mr. Hyer was older than I and in some business ways more experienced. I did not have to observe him very long before I could see that he had the makings of a great merchant.

When I suggested, the following spring, that he take charge of the Walla Walla store, with a third interest, he hesitated. It seemed strange to him, he said later, that a man could give a third interest in a going concern without requiring substantial investment of capital. My proposition was that he pay for his third interest out of earnings.

After thinking it over— "getting the hang" of our partnership philosophy, so to speak—he accepted. He managed the store most successfully until a few years later, when we established the St. Louis office, where he was given charge of the shoe department. At about the same time he was made a director of the J. C. Penney Company and has so remained ever since.

It always has seemed to me that Wilk Hyer was able to train so many good men as he has for the company because he sold them lastingly our interpretation of honor and integrity. Many times in our long association it has come to me that he embodies what I call the "foursquare man." Through the powers of purpose, integrity, service, and faith in the Divine, the foursquare man liberates the best within himself and others, directing it to the accomplishing of constructive good. When a man is foursquare in business and all his other human dealings and relationships, he becomes foursquare with his Creator, who endowed him to render service to his fellow-men.

We older men in the organization spent our time actively in the field, putting our experience at the service of those coming along. As Mr. Callahan and Mr. Johnson had taken me to market, we took younger men to the wholesale centers, pooling time and practical experience for the common interest.

Day by day we were infiltrating the organization with evidence that standards of merchandising could be as high as those of any profession. The idea of partnership was dynamic and encompassing. Not only our store managers but the communities served were partners. Our formula comprised a basic liking for human beings, plus integrity, plus industry, plus creative imagination expressing itself in the capacity to see the other fellow's point of view.

I have noticed that, when business principles are explained to some people, they complain of intellectual meagerness. Yet such people would not, when a chemist explained the formula for water as two parts hydrogen and one part oxygen, complain that the formula lacks sophistication. No one protests that the physicist's explanation of the laws of leverage lack originality. Why, then, do basic truths in the field of merchandising seem too commonplace?

The six principles I adopted at Kemmerer are to me old-fashioned—just as old-fashioned as the golden rule, which, if you stop to think of it, is also as new-fashioned as tomorrow morning.

These are the principles:

*Preparation Wins.* A man must know all about his business. He must know a little more than any other man knows. As a rule we achieve what we prepare for.

*Hard Work Wins.* The only kind of luck that any man is justified in banking on is hard work, which is made up of sacrifice, persistent effort, and dogged determination. Growth is never by mere chance. The success we build will be the achievement of our united efforts.

*Honesty Wins.* This must be not only the kind of honesty that keeps a man's fingers out of his neighbor's till, but the finer honesty that will not allow a man to give less than his best, the kind of honesty that makes him count not his hours but his duties and opportunities, and constantly urges him to increase his efficiency.

*Confidence in Men Wins.* I have found my most successful associates by giving men responsibility, by making them feel that I relied upon them; and those who have proved to be unworthy have only caused the others, who far outnumbered them, to stand in a clearer light. This principle, at least in a measure, is responsible for the success of our mercantile organization. Use good business judgment, of course. Do not throw away common sense, but believe in yourself, and trust your fellows.

*The Spirit Wins.* One of the wisest men who ever lived said, "The letter killeth, the spirit giveth life." Every enterprise I have been interested in demonstrates this fact. It is the spirit of the individuals comprising any organization, the spirit of the pioneers in any enterprise or endeavor—that spirit of men and women who are at the foundation of such organizations and enterprises—which will solve problems, conquer difficulties, and achieve individual and collective successes.

*A Practical Application of the Golden Rule Wins.* As enunciated by the Master Teacher on the hillsides of Judea nearly two thousand years ago, the golden rule runs, "Therefore all things whatsoever ye would that men should do to you, do ye even so to them; for this is the law and the prophets."

After two years of increasingly complex direction of the growing chain I was still haunted by the feeling that if I could just go far away for a while—search for the meaning of life— I could get my bearings again.

Throughout the time since my wife's death Dr. Short had stood by me in a most sympathetic and undersanding way. With rare and sensitive tact he had tried to prevail on me to come into the church fellowship. The fact that I was not yet ready within myself expressed itself in various ways. I told myself that people might say I was becoming a church mem-

ber for effect, to add prestige to my business position. It was
such a poor, frivolous excuse that the reader will comprehend
just how unready I really was, inwardly, to take the step of
relinquishing my will to God.

I proposed to Dr. Short that together we take a trip abroad.
In some groping way I believed that, by visiting Europe,
Egypt, Palestine, the Holy Land, somehow I might draw
closer to the presence of God. I took my two boys, Roswell,
aged ten, and J. C., Jr., aged seven, along with us.

Of course the real trouble was that, foolishly, I was pre-
suming to make the terms on which God could have me,
instead of letting Him make the terms on which He would
take my life and make it His. It was a bad approach to a relationship with God and could not have succeeded.

# CHAPTER EIGHT

On the trip Dr. Short and I also had the company of Newell Beaman, a retired Evanston merchant whom I thought a a great deal of.

From the outset the trip was invaluable to me on one count alone. Dr. Short was a gifted scholar as well as a good friend, and in long shipboard and overland talks he gave me generous access to his knowledge and wisdom.

In appearance he was a sort of blond giant, with strong features and striking blue eyes. He had an inquiring and fearless mind and an outspoken but eminently fair point of view.

Out of his superior knowledge of the Bible, with skill he lifted many meanings clear for me which had been hidden, illuminated many points which, in my limitation, I had judged to be inconsistencies in the Bible.

In the Holy Land we made our way through the very streets and lanes, crosscuts and bypaths where Jesus and His associates walked. The thought impressed me, what countless miles these men *walked,* to bring to mankind the message of Security.

Dr. Short did not so much try to convert me. As we traveled he sought rather to distract my mind from destructive thinking, to help me find the rest and mental relaxation which change of scene should bring. He had wisdom to comprehend, as the Gospel according to St. Mark records, that the law of Nature is "First the blade, then the ear, after that the full corn in the ear."

Yet many of my deeper questions were slow of solving. What was the purpose of life, its true meaning? What was the reason behind my loss, the deep discontent within me, refusing to be quieted, untouched even by material success which was coming to me in undreamed-of abundance?

Making money, the accumulation of material wealth, though well enough as far as it went, was—or should be— a means, rather than end; a foundation on which to rear a structure of larger life. But in my present state of mind it was difficult to envision a larger life.

It was perhaps natural that my mind whiled away time in relating what I saw to the world of business. Looking back from the shores of Europe, from the Pyramids keeping their endless vigil, from the ancient terraces of the Jerusalem hills, I pondered the periods of human history wherein distribution of goods as a practical science had been overlooked and neglected, and how such neglect had been visited on the lives of people.

Even countries fairly advanced in production techniques struggled ineffectually, with millions who were unemployed for no reason but that badly distributed wealth prevented the mass of people from purchasing what could be produced. Everywhere peasants and wage-earners alike were attempting with energy and realism to reduce the cost of distribution to the consumer, through co-operatives; but nowhere was there evidence of a real technique of fast mass distribution, at low unit cost and low unit profit, by rapid flow of huge quantities of goods through channels of trade serving the mutual advantage of both distributor and consumer.

As we traveled from the north of Europe toward the Mediterranean I observed how the channels of distribution from the great industrial centers gradually diminished, practically disappearing altogether before the Near East could be reached.

Local distribution in the Near East struck me as having progressed little or none since the great plundering days of Genghis Khan. The standard of average living in 1913 was pitiably low. There were the eternally poisonous seeds of war in this bad relation between production and distribution of goods, these immoderate concentrations of wealth in certain geographical areas while great economic blanks persisted elsewhere.

In terms of what I saw on every side I secured a whole new sense of the possibilities and everyday human advantages of such a distributive system as was evolving from the beginnings at Kemmerer, in turn based on the kernel of an idea with which Mr. Callahan and Mr. Johnson had first stirred my independent energy and sense of pioneering adventure in Evanston.

In Europe I got the feel of the massive pent-up urge which literally drove great numbers of human beings to cross the Atlantic Ocean, and the Appalachian chain, daring prairie, desert, mountain range, to break their bonds of slavery to outmoded social and economic ways.

Such people, hungry for land and the liberty to make their

own better, earned way of life, had built and were building
the towns in which my associates and I were building stores.
These were tillers of the soil, miners, farmers, herders, but,
above all, they were freedom-seeking pioneers. Where they
had come others were following. By their swift dispersion,
from narrow, archaic environments, they were creating an
incalculable demand for basic goods over a territory rivaling
the whole of Europe in area, and where as yet there were
no modern facilities for bringing them goods of quality in
quantity.

It struck me that, as merchants, we too ranked as pioneers.
We too were spreading out. Already we had laid down the
beginnings of swift transmission lines, between our community stores and the great sources of supply in the manufactur-
ing cities of the East.

As our outlets spread, and resources permitted, we would
develop new outlets. Much as had railroads, and telephone
and telegraph systems, in a foreseeable future we could become a national entity.

It was in the Holy Land, as spring was coming on, that I
grasped a great truth: it is useless to run away from life,
which must rather be faced fairly and squarely. Out of recognizing that principle a quieting sense of self-renewal seemed
to come to me. I felt on more solid ground again, prepared
to stop running away, to go home and begin again.

We booked passage and began the journey to England and
the port city.

A distant event shocked us. On April 14, in a North
Atlantic sea lane, an iceberg loomed suddenly from a no-

where of fog. The White Star liner *Titanic,* in that lane on maiden voyage, collided with the fearful ice-blue mass and sank, with a loss of 1517 souls.

It was a matter for pondering, that we had been booked to sail from Liverpool on the *Titanic's* second voyage.

# CHAPTER NINE

When I returned from Europe the decision was taken to change the name to "J. C. Penney Company" from "Golden Rule Store." Personally I felt reluctant to make the change, because "Golden Rule" was far more than just a name to me; it had a definite significance in relation to the operation of the stores. But the judgment of my associates prevailed. Incidentally, it was Mr. Sams' turn to smile; because the term was abused in many quarters, or at best passively interpreted, from the time he joined me in Kemmerer he had disbelieved in our using it.

It was also clear that we should incorporate all the stores in one company.

I plunged into the complex problem of establishing large credits in New York. The intricacy of financial detail is not relevant here; but after the incorporation the situation was as follows:

The company, per se, owned no stock. Classified stock was issued to the partners in proportion to their store interests, and dividends were paid against earnings of each store, distributed according to individual holdings in each store.

Directors had authority to oversee opening of new stores and/or to discontinue existing stores. Costs of liquidation were paid by owners of stores discontinued.

Partners remained free to train new men and open new stores out of earnings, continuing to participate in the earnings of these new stores. The *partnership idea*, lifeblood of our enterprise. stood unimpaired.

To me the sacredness of the partnership idea is well illustrated in a discussion, at a meeting of store managers, of centralized buying and the training of what I felt were necessary specialists in use of credit, trade discounts, and kindred matters. The majority of partners were inclined to be reluctant, basically because the warehouse in Salt Lake City had not worked out, and offices in New York would seem pretty distant. I had figures, however, to prove wasted time and money under the existing method. Still, they would have none of them.

In an effort to find through an impartial view any blind spot in my reasoning, I talked the matter over informally with a banker friend. He was inclined to concur with the partners; but, knowing that I felt strongly in favor of the change, he said, "Well, Mr. Penney, since you own a majority of stock, in view of the way you feel, why don't you just go ahead and do as you please? You can compel your partners to go along on it."

"Compel them?" I exclaimed. "Oh no, I couldn't do that!"

"Why not?"

"A man can't *compel* his partners."

"Not if you know they're wrong and you're right?"

"Still unthinkable," I said.

It puzzled my friend. He said, "I simply can't understand your basis of reasoning."

"My point of view is simply that partners are men working

as one, instead of as several. Everything we believe about what we are building is rooted in our concept of partnership. It is much more important that the partnership idea be kept intact than that I should make—or force—any point of mine." The action subsequently taken was an action by partners.

If I had insisted on keeping personal control of the Penney Company we would still be merely a small chain of stores scattered through the Middle West. The real growth came after the incorporation.

My earlier plan of setting up a warehouse in Salt Lake City, to hold goods bought by one general drygoods buyer for all member-stores, had contained a flaw. The flaw was hiring an outside man as buyer. He and the store managers spoke a different language. Our type of store buying was a special process and had to be done by someone equipped to understand and speak the language of the manager of each individual store.

It is odd that I should have made such a slip because when I was with Johnson & Callahan an incident had occurred which bore directly on the value of primary operation of all functions involved in the business.

Mr. Johnson and Mr. Callahan took me to New York on a buying trip. We went to a wholesale house to look at piece goods. I asked for samples, which I took back with me to the hotel.

Alone in my room that night I washed every one of the samples with soap in the washbasin, pinning them on the window curtains to dry.

Mr. Callahan dropped in on some errand, and when he saw

my strange laundry he cried, "Jim, what under the sun are you doing?"

"I have to find out for myself whether or not these goods are fast color," I said.

"But you heard me question the wholesaler on that very point! He says the colors are fast."

"Mr. Callahan, I'm the one who has to tell the customers that the colors are fast. Before I can tell them, I have to know. If I don't know, why should customers trust anything I tell them?"

He shook his head. "Jim, if you're going to spend your time doing things like this, you'll just never get to be a big merchant."

The thought in my mind was that I must be a good merchant. If I were a good merchant, the rest would probably take care of itself. I made it a business practice to collect the knowledge which would make my word to customers good.

In the end we liquidated the Salt Lake City warehouse. However, to me it was the attempt which failed, rather than the idea. I have another reason for not considering it a loss without some gain. The incident led to a long-standing association with a man named George H. Bushnell. First Mr. Bushnell helped with the inventory which was the preliminary step to liquidation of the warehouse. Then he helped to install a centralized bookkeeping, accounting, and over-all financing system.

When I first ran across him Mr. Bushnell was employed by a farm implement firm, in Ogden. He was an accountant, and traveled most of the time.

One night I was in our store in Preston, working late. Mr.

Bushnell happened to be passing by; he noticed the lights and thought he'd drop in on someone who worked as late hours as he did. We had a casual conversation, mostly about the stores and how the partnership idea worked.

After that when he happened to be in Preston he fell into the habit of dropping in on the manager of the Golden Rule Store. One night the manager asked Mr. Bushnell what share he owned in the farm implement business.

"None," said Mr. Bushnell. "I just work on salary."

"That's a surprise; you work such long hours that I thought sure you must have an interest in the business, like myself." He added something to the effect that some day he might have something to talk about which would interest Mr. Bushnell.

The next time I ran into Mr. Bushnell we were both waiting for a train at two o'clock in the morning at Pocatello, Idaho. I made it a rule never to spend money on a hotel for a small part of a night. It interested me that Bushnell had the same rule, to save his employer money.

There wasn't any fire in the railroad station, and only the dim light from an oil lamp. The thermometer stood at forty below zero. But we passed the time agreeably, talking about our business experiences.

Some time earlier I had employed John I. H. Herbert as auditor for all the stores in which I had investments. Herbert would need someone to help take inventory in advance of the warehouse liquidation. I thought George Bushnell would make us a good man.

I wrote him, outlining an idea for his coming down to us in Salt Lake City. Our work would probably not keep him as

busy as he would need to be, but I thought he could get some
night work on the side. For our work I would pay him $80.00
a month.

"I'm getting $175.00 a month and considerable expenses,"
he wrote back. "I appreciate your letter, but can't quite see
my way to a drop to $80.00 a month salary."

I have had a fixed belief from the beginning of my career
that, if a man can't see how to come to us for less than he is
getting where he is, he doesn't have a very clear insight into
the big opportunities of our partnership plan.

I might just digress here to an illustration of this which
comes to mind, though it was some years later.

When I first knew him, the President of the Penney Company A. W. Hughes was the Latin instructor at the Hill
School in Pottstown, Pennsylvania. For two summers he
tutored my two boys and two nephews.

In my library he came across a complete file of the company
magazine *Dynamo,* and didn't stop until he had read every
issue. Then he came to me. "I'm going to quit schoolteaching,
Mr. Penney," he said, "and I want a job with the Penney
Company."

He was getting a good salary at Hill School. I said, "We
couldn't afford to pay you more than $100 a month, or per-
haps even $75."

"I haven't said anything about the money, Mr. Penney. I
just like the idea of the company, and want a job with it."

When I saw that he couldn't be discouraged from going
through with his idea, I sent him to the store which John
Weber had in Moberly, Missouri. When it was time for him

to step up his training, he was sent to Eureka, Utah, Mr. Sams' first store.

In those years we had a tryout period for the managers. Mr. Hughes knew that he had made a good showing and was looking forward to a very complimentary letter from headquarters.

In looking over his record I felt that it was a little too good. So Mr. Sams wrote him a letter in which he asked him to think over whether perhaps he had made too much money, whether his profits weren't abnormally large, because of a bigger than normal markup on merchandise. "This isn't the way we do things in the Penney Company," the letter said. "We owe to our community the service of merchandise at a fair profit. We can't ever allow ourselves to make too much profit. Somewhere, in doing the most business ever done in Eureka, and making the most money ever made there I believe there is some profit that we owe to our public rather than ourselves. I am not censuring you; I would just like you to think my suggestions over and let me know what you think."

After he thought it over Mr. Hughes agreed with us, making up his mind to pay closer attention to the principle involved.

The point I am making in recalling this incident is that, like many men who made sacrifices to come with the Penney Company, Mr. Hughes was looking for a place in which to express God-given powers, a future rather than immediate security.

Going back to Mr. Bushnell: Once I made a man an offer

I seldom raised it. It has always been against my policy to make salary the primary inducement. But in Mr. Bushnell's case I decided there were some special factors, and I wrote him again.

"Well then, I will pay you $90.00. When may I expect you to report?"

Mr. Bushnell often told people about it later. He and his wife owned their home in Ogden; all their friends were there. My offer still seemed rather outlandish to them yet in a curious way they felt drawn to it. So they kept on considering it.

Mr. Bushnell began sounding out others. One of his friends, a state senator, told him that he knew Guy Johnson and Mr. Callahan well, and knew *about* me. "I think you'd work into a good position if you connect up with the J. C. Penney Company, and I advise you to do it."

So he wrote me that he would try to sell his home, come to Salt Lake City, and see what happened. For some reason I didn't confirm his letter immediately, and he went to Salt Lake to see me, but I wasn't there. Faced with having to decide what to do he went back to Ogden, resigned a job he had held for nearly eight years, just pulled up stakes, and reported to the J. C. Penney Company office in Salt Lake City, on an autumn day in 1911.

I have always remembered with gratitude this clear evidence of faith in the partnership idea and in me. Mr. Bushnell had very little in the way of a definite prospect to go on; not even as much, really, as men who entered our stores as clerks. But he felt the inspiration to take his chance with an idea; it was the beginning of a satisfying and fruitful association all around.

In addition to the name and other changes initiated after my return from Europe I decided that it was time to resume the idea of a central buying office, with warehousing facilities, this time in New York. In view of losses resulting from the earlier venture at Salt Lake City it was natural that my partners should hesitate about establishing another warehouse. This time I proceeded with double care.

My selection of the trainee, and working with him, was, in miniature, an example of what I came to believe represented my best service to the growing company, namely the selection and training of men endowed with the kind of vision and the practical capacity to carry on the building process of "a chain of dry goods stores that will cover these mountain states."

Although I said nothing about this to Mr. Sams or other associates I had decided in my own mind that, when the central buying headquarters in New York was at last working efficiently, I would step down as President of the Company.

I chose a trainee from the ranks, and took him to New York for the training period at my own expense. The partners objected to my bearing the entire cost, but I was glad to have it that way while we worked out the project, on the basis of my experience with markets and buying, and the trainee's experience with J. C. Penney Company manager's standards for merchandise.

In 1914 this aspect was developed to a point where it could be taken over by the company. At desk room in my small New

York office the whole foundation was prepared for what, not so long afterward, became the buying headquarters of the entire J. C. Penney Company.

In the twelve years since I had started in Kemmerer in business for myself I had seen the hold of the company stores broken in a number of places. There was no sense of triumph in seeing loss come to a competitor; rather, it was gratifying that the point had been made, *Better merchandise for cash*. By our standards of service and value the true spirit of the golden rule was being spread. The nature of our stores and philosophy was some sort of landmark in the history of business, and it was a satisfaction that the Penney Company was becoming known as the one to shed a bright, clean light. We had started out with an idea, a willingness to put it to work—and to allow it to put us to work too!—and the determination to keep it working, in greater and greater measure.

We denied ourselves many a convenience and refinement of storekeeping for the furtherance of the greater goal. It was not an empty complaint when Mr. Sams commented that the stores had a certain "junky" look. Later this all came to be changed, but in the early years merchandise was displayed wherever it would catch the customer's eye: red woolen socks hung from rings; bandannas, suspenders, rubber boots, long underwear, corsets, wrappers hung from the ceiling and even outside the stores—anything to make the customer conscious of the size and variety of stock.

When Mr. Bushnell and Mr. Herbert were working out the consolidated statement system which, with a revised warehouse plan, was part of my plans in 1911, they noted the leanness of our office equipment. The office was a room, about 30 x 35, with a cement floor, one flat-top desk (loaned me by a friend), and one old-fashioned standing desk, which shrewd merchants of an earlier day had devised on the principle that a bookkeeper who has to stand up to do his work will not be very likely to fall asleep and waste time.

I slit the envelopes of my mail, using the blank sides for scratch paper. We didn't have a typewriter but did all work in longhand. When a pencil was needed, one of us went out and bought it for a penny. We bought ink a bottle at a time, as we did penholders, with pen points by the nickel's worth, as we absolutely had to have them.

By 1914, with the central buying headquarters in operation, I wanted to get away from administrative and executive detail and concentrate on becoming, so to speak, a fisher of men.

To expand in a framework of security each link in the chain must meet the standard of the best, and each manager must be helped not only to make the most of his own business opportunities but so to train the men under him that each store would be increasingly a source of new manager material.

To learn our business thoroughly and operate it successfully there would never be any substitute for hard work. Long hours of *thinking, planning, doing;* character, discipline and self-denial, and close application to the job were minimal requirements. There was no place for guesswork, for we wanted every man who came with us to succeed.

Our Kemmerer rule-of-thumb practices had, by 1914, been codified, so to speak, into an instrument which we referred to among ourselves as "The Original Body of Doctrine." Later the components, wording unchanged, came to be known as "Penney Principles."

These principles were and are:

1. To serve the public, as nearly as we can, to its complete satisfaction.

2. To offer the best possible dollar's worth of quality and value.

3. To strive constantly for a high level of intelligent and helpful service.

4. To charge a fair profit for what we offer—and not all the traffic will bear.

5. To apply this test to everything we do: "Does it square with what is right and just?"

The kind of men I wanted to discover in increasing numbers would see our stores as oases of contiguous serving.

Basically the stores were places where the folks of a town and its outlying regions could buy needed goods. For us to stay in a position to sell always at lowest possible prices we had to work constantly. We had to save, not only in prices paid in the wholesale markets, but on costs all along the line right to shelves and over the counter. Stocks must turn over down to the last paper of pins a given number of times in a year. By our service to our customers we would create in them that spring of sparkling good will which would prompt them to want to help *us* to serve *them*.

It might not always be convenient or pleasant for them to carry packages instead of having them delivered. But part of our service lay in making packages so neat and tidy that they wouldn't seriously mind carrying them because they under-stood that the carrying permitted us to keep expenses of doing business to a minimum, and that savings—far from being used to line our own pockets—were passed on to our customers, in the real golden rule way.

From the beginning my experience in storekeeping taught me that *little things*—the atoms in the molecule of the principle—mark both good salesmen and good service.

Speaking of little things, I remember visiting one day in one of the Kansas stores. I had inspected it and was in conversation with the manager and several others when I noticed a parcel being wrapped by a clerk. I sensed that something about it wanted improvement.

When the customer had gone, I asked the clerk to show me a shirt. He handed it to me and I rolled it up and wrapped it into a small, tight package and then unrolled it again, saying, "You see, this is the wrinkled shirt the customer will find when he undoes his parcel at home. What will he think of this purchase then?" I explained to him carefully that a shirt should be wrapped flat, taking particular care that the collar is not mussed. There is a natural tendency for a man to put on a new shirt as soon as possible, which he cannot do if it has been wrapped so the collar is mussed.

With each sale we have two chances to make a good impression on the customer: one when we present to him in the store clean, attractive stock to buy; the other when the parcel is opened at home and the favorable impression created in the store is confirmed, generating the will to return to trade with us again, and again, and again, until doing so becomes a regular habit.

In order that I might give my full attention to the selection and training of men, Mr. Sams became President of the J. C. Penney Company on January 1, 1917. His selection expressed the choice of all the managers, meeting in convention, as well as my own. I became Chairman of the Board.

One factor seemed to me particularly important, in yield-the presidency. I believed the spirit of the partnership plan could, conceivably, be handicapped by allowing the implication to take hold in partners' minds—or, for that matter, in my own mind—that I was indispensable. Any such mistaken notion would, in its essence, contradict my conviction that men whom I selected and trained were then capable of discharging any responsibility their associates might place on them. You see, the faith, the freedom of initiative reposed in me by Mr. Callahan and Mr. Johnson in sending me to Kemmerer, was ever in my mind. Nothing must be allowed to impede the steady flow throughout our organization of this incentive.

Four months after Mr. Sams became President there was a development related to company policy which, incidentally, had a rather far-reaching effect on me. In April, 1917, fifteen years after I opened the Kemmerer store, the first issue of *The Dynamo,* a company house organ, was published.

Basically *The Dynamo's* purpose was to put into the hands of every member of the organization a working kit of facts, ideas, and suggestions which, hitherto, my older associates and I had been in the habit of carrying around in person to the stores. We wanted a conveyor belt whereby the experiences of all could flow evenly and regularly to all.

It was not particularly difficult to put on the printed page the foundation principles, history of the organization, and fundamentals of right storekeeping. It was rather more of a problem to make the magazine a medium for the exchange of day-to-day experiences in the stores, with assurance that it would serve also as a handbook, kept up to date month by month for practical use.

Like myself, the majority of our associates had had limited schooling. Rather they were people of action, not readers, and relatively few—even as I—expressed themselves clearly in writing.

It had been a rule with me from the start of my business life to expect no more of others than I demanded of myself. As I read manuscripts submitted for *The Dynamo,* and looked further into its potential as a textbook of J. C. Penney store development, it seemed to me we were falling short of the mark.

As the first step in getting at a solution I took inventory of my own capacities, therefore. My facility with English was weak, noticeably in the written word.

It was an old deficiency. Once, as a boy, I had,—like most boys—"published a newspaper," the items being written in pencil on brown wrapping paper. I sent a complimentary copy to our justice of the peace. He went to some trouble to point out my mistakes in punctuation, and his literary criticism was considerable. The newspaper soon went the way of a boy's world but I often pondered the justice's estimate of my English and use of commas and semicolons—or lack of them!

I had only to look back at copies of business letters, among them those to Mr. Sams, to admit that. I had little aptitude with textbooks, so how could I expect to infuse effective textbook properties in *The Dynamo?*

In the light of my own deficiencies it struck me that what was needed was contact with the type of mind having not only a large grasp of culture but the capacity also to render that grasp into educational material which would guide, stimulate, and broaden the human practices of small-town storekeeping.

In an almost laughably incidental way I found my man.

# CHAPTER TEN

In New York the J. C. Penney Company now had its office in a building on Seventh Avenue. On the same floor Platt & Peck, a book concern, rented a showroom and sales space. One day, just passing by, I dropped in to look over the books on the counter and picked up one by a man named Dr. Thomas Tapper called *Youth and Opportunity*.

When I read it the book made such an impression on me that I inquired of the bookstore proprietor where I could meet the author. The proprietor arranged a meeting, and we three had lunch at the Manhattan Hotel. As Dr. Tapper remembers it now, about the only time I spoke during lunch was to ask his opinion of some printing on a pamphlet which I showed him. He remarked frankly, "I think it's about the worst job of the kind I ever saw."

In November I telephoned him. At the time he was lecturing at several institutions, in the Departments of Music and the Fine Arts, and also on the science of personnel, and business efficiency. It was his somewhat rare combination of talents which arrested my attention.

On the telephone I said, "I don't suppose you remember me." Purposely I did not give my name.

"You're J. C. Penney," he said at once. It was another

talent of his—remembering voices, and the people and names that went with them.

I was turning over in my mind a solution for a combination of problems; both my own shortcomings of education and the shaping of a course of reading and study to which Penney personnel could have free access, and which I felt convinced could be made of constructive benefit all along the line.

Whereas many well-educated men can regard with excitement Stradivarius' way of making a violin, or the inspired way in which two French dyers, the brothers Gilles and Jehan Gobelin, colored materials with which they and their descendants originated unique and incomparably beautiful tapestries, it is sometimes more difficult for them to perceive the connection between culture and the making and selling of everyday merchandise. Yet are not all arts, cultures, religions related to utilitarian activities? Culture and the exchange of goods, comprising the commerce of the world, are connected at many points.

In keeping with my considered and long-standing rule not to require more of my associates than of myself, before asking Penney personnel to avail themselves of any special reading-and-study plan I proposed first to follow it myself as a student. Too, having grown up in the habit of expecting no aid except my own powers, in the same spirit of depending on myself for power I felt the need of organizing latent personal resources. In the long view I wanted to see a curriculum set up for general use, but first I intended to go through it myself. The object of such a curriculum would be to find undeveloped resources.

From the time I finished high school I had not been much

of a reader. I really had no time for anything so essentially sedentary as reading. It is true that one feature of the first issue of *The Dynamo* (a feature we continued, finding it achieved a good effect) did connect with a minor reading habit which I pursued during my Wyoming and Utah days. Incidentally, it had to do with the only good thing (so far as I am concerned) which ever came out of a pack of cigarettes.

As a promotion item one cigarette company enclosed in its package a picture card, bearing a portrait and brief biography of a famous American. These thumb nail sketches of Presidents, writers, painters, men and women of many achievements, could be assimilated almost at a glance. They were factually interesting and well written. We adapted them to *The Dynamo* to the extent of including in each issue a biographical sketch of a man who had achieved notable success in some field other than our own. Years later I learned that the series distributed in the cigarette packs marked the first writing commission of Dutch-born Edward Bok.

In addition to the broad educational opportunity represented by a well-devised reading-and-study plan for Penney personnel as a whole, I was moved by a personal practical consideration. The J. C. Penney Company was beginning to attract considerable attention in the business and financial worlds. A rising, successful merchant is called on from time to time to make speeches and give interviews to the trade and newspaper press. All too well I knew that I possessed neither the knowledge nor the finish to respond effectively to such calls. I felt a distinct need to learn to write clearly, to speak acceptably in public, and to become, all round, a better-read man.

Accordingly, I proposed that Dr. Tapper should take me in hand and tutor me. I took a room in Aeolian Hall where we would be able to work in quiet. For eighteen months I worked half of every business day, reading and writing under his direction. Nothing was permitted to break the appointments. One of my most fixed habits is store visiting, but throughout those eighteen months I hardly went out on the road at all. Those months were among the richest and most stimulating of my life.

I made slow work of the reading at first. But soon it became such an exciting adventure to me that I wondered why, in high school back in Hamilton, I had never had the sheer sense of discovery in reading and appreciation of great books. Dr. Tapper's assignments to me ran from Plato to Ruskin and Thackeray. I wrote reports on what I read, and discussed with him the structure of the reports, the correctness of my interpretations or lack of it.

Dr. Tapper encouraged me by explaining that instinctively active men are almost never naturally word-minded. They become habituated, *by doing,* to talking and reading little.

He would cite to me such examples as Gladstone, and Sir John Lubbock (Baron Avebury), who wrote important books and did important things but talked with difficulty. Though Gladstone did speak, he was ever a man of slow, if pregnant, expression. Phillips Brooks could talk—if the subject were in the realm of the spiritual. On the whole, Dr. Tapper encouraged me to see that the greater a man's responsibilities the less spontaneous was his articulation likely to be. But such men could nearly always be helped, if they truly wished to increase facility.

When I first suggested to Dr. Tapper that he relinquish his activities as music critic and lecturer to do educational work for a retail drygoods organization, he was somewhat doubtful that such an organization would, in the nature of its own activity, be able to utilize an educational plan of high quality. However, I continued to urge on him that he come with us, and before long he agreed to do so. He later told me that Mrs. Tapper had such a clear perception of what we aimed to do that she resolved his lingering doubts.

As my own study course matured, Dr. Tapper and I began, therefore, to visit stores together. Attending store meetings we observed how they were organized and conducted by the managers or their first men. Some acted with facility; others fumbled, were awkward and inclined to be shy and embarrassed. When someone to whom a subject had been assigned was absent, because of sickness or some other unexpected reason, there was likely to be a troublesome gap.

This bore a relation to one of our most important structural factors. In our manager-partnership plan the manager must, first of all, be a leader and trainer of men, not solely for the efficiency of the parent store but because new stores could only be opened, new opportunities created for promotion, as men could be trained to take advantage of them. In the Penney Company men never have been hired as managers; they have always developed inside the company.

It came to me that the difference between an educated and an uneducated person is explained, not by a difference in advantages, but in *the will to do*. Too, it was never our thought primarily to train men *to work;* rather to train them *to serve,* willingly and intelligently. It is not really creative to train men merely to obey orders, which they may or may not fully understand. Train them rather to study the job, to develop perception in relation to what is to be done, then to apply to it their understanding, initiative, and effort.

On the basis of our trips Dr. Tapper prepared a *Store Meeting Manual,* designed to augment *The Dynamo,* with specific directions for conducting all phases of a meeting, topical outlines for general store meetings, and technical outlines for men's meetings, through each month of the year. Each publication complemented the other, *The Dynamo* carrying case material relating to outlines in the manual.

From the first, my ultimate hope for *The Dynamo* was that it would be a source book of case material, connecting with correspondence courses touching everything pertinent, from the inherent meaning of our foundation principles to selling merchandise across the counter.

It did appear to me that, by helping a man to help himself, you tie him to you in such a way that he would never desert you. On the other hand, there never was anything compulsory about an educational procedure. Character comes out in the exercise of initiative, and we did not see the courses as anything to be forced on associates. Neither did we look for maximum effectuality overnight. The essence of the educational idea, applying to our stores, was creative, and would therefore take time to find its place. The training program and literature sent out were, from the first, designed simply and solely to help. *Doing* is up to the individual. I was interested only in a plan which would call forth individual latent powers. As a merchant committed to observance of the golden rule as the cornerstone and first principle of my business, I interpreted the golden rule as the sharing of profits, and training other men to be merchants who would, in turn, share profits. So long as we stood bound to that principle we, as partners, knew our stores were not in danger from any outside force. In sharing profits, not only within our partner group but with the public, by selling at lower prices, we could be confident that old customers would come back, and new customers would constantly join them.

Not since I started business in Kemmerer has anyone figured aggregate dollar savings to J. C. Penney Store customers. Very likely they would total in the hundreds of millions of dollars. Too, there is unquestionably an enormous factor of indirect savings: factories kept open by large Penney Store orders, placed in what otherwise would be a slack, or even closed-door, period; merchants who have enjoyed better business owing to the "traffic" of a Penney store in their midst.

These are our own evidences that the golden rule and storekeeping are mutually workable, where the golden rule is envisioned in the well-being of the people who walk into a Penney store, and its dealings with them.

No educational process can be fixed. In its nature it must constantly change, improve, adjust to circumstances and human beings in proportion as they react to the evolutionary changes of a business. From the days at Kemmerer I have sincerely believed that the best education for young men and women in business derives from the demands made upon them *by the job itself*. To analyze and comprehend the elements of the job, then to make them the basis of constructive study for advancement, is to accord education of high quality a natural place in business, recognizing its equality in influence with other integral activities.

Through the association with Dr. Tapper I gained insight in many directions. The way he went about the shaping of our educational materials pointed up for me the essential folly of attempting to go unprepared into a thing. This had a delayed relation to a mistake of my own. The butcher-shop venture was a substantial example of folly. I knew nothing about running a butcher shop and did not take the time to learn. The resulting experience taught me three fundamental lessons:

Don't resort to expedients.

Don't compromise.

Don't go into something you know nothing about.

I had an even more personal reason for appreciating the contact wih Dr. Tapper's uncommon and clear-thinking personality. Although I had to some extent, since returning from Europe, risen above the awful weight of depression that overwhelmed me as a result of losing the wife who was so intimately a part of my aspirations, I was by no means entirely free of it. But one incident connected with Dr. Tapper made a lasting impression on me. It had to do with the loss of his own wife.

I was waiting for him to come downstairs, in a room where the shades were drawn. Entering the room he walked directly to the windows and raised the shades, to let in a flood of heartening sunshine. "There's no need now for gloom," he remarked, with simplicity. More than anything perhaps that had ever been said to me before, this one sentence,—"There's no need for gloom,—" showed me that by persistent grieving we only harm ourselves.

From my observation of the personalities and dominant characteristics of our Salt Lake City pastor, Dr. Short, and Dr. Tapper, the idea grew on me that, education-wise, in relation to the J. C. Penney Company, they would make a dynamic team.

Dr. Short had moved from Salt Lake City to Spokane, and I often saw him there. To him I was indebted for grounding me in a wise and enlightened philosophy of giving of my means, to churches, schools, hospitals and so on.

Mrs. Short was one of the very best cooks I ever ran across, and whenever I was in Spokane of a Sunday I was sure of an invitation to dinner, for it was known that I was partial to her stewed chicken and dumplings.

One Sunday when I was there Dr. Short said to me suddenly after dinner, "Penney, do you want to know what I think of you?" I had a high regard for him and his estimates of people, and naturally felt eager to hear. Besides, the rather human thought occurred to me that, since I was a guest in his house, what he had to say would in all probability be complimentary!

"In all my experience," he said, "I have never seen a man with such contradictory characteristics as I see in you. You can drive a bargain as relentlessly as any man I've ever seen —and then turn around squarely and give an equivalent amount away—and more too." As a compliment it was somewhat unusual; but I chose to take it as an indication that he granted the sincerity of my desire to practice the golden rule consistently.

While Dr. Short remained in the church at Spokane he became more and more concerned that I should enter church membership. He did not have any patience with my apprehension that some might infer that I—known to be a hard-headed businessman—was making a gesture, for effect on the community. He urged me earnestly to look on it rather as a step which would make what he generously regarded as my great influence "immeasurably greater." Once he wired to remind me that he would gladly come across the country to New York to receive me into the church on Easter Sunday, if I should so desire.

But the process of change within me was still far from complete.

In the light of later evaluation there is no question that my motivations in those years remained predominantly ethical rather than spiritual. As always, I was concerned with a strictly upright pattern of life; that was the way I had been raised; it never occurred to me to change. As for the religious expression, to which I had been equally conditioned, it is clear that, as the absorptions of expanding success, making money, gripped me, with the accompanying excitement of business adventure, which can become highly captivating, I was permitting the forms of religious expression to fade more and more into the background of my living.

But with reference to Dr. Short, it did seem to me that he had qualities which could be of inspiring service to the J. C. Penney Company, and, in turn, that the J. C. Penney Company could afford him an enlarged field of service to his fellow-man.

We therefore invited him to join our now quite well-oriented educational department. There followed a varied, rich, and fruitful association. As I expected, he and Dr. Tapper made a superb team, each possessing talents which were complementary.

Dr. Short traveled all over the country, filling speaking engagements in the store towns, and elsewhere where people had an interest in hearing about principles and the testing of them in ways which had contributed not only to the growth of our particular company but, we liked to think, to the golden rule concept applied to the broad aspects of doing business, under conditions of individual initiative.

Some fifteen years ago, not long before Dr. Short passed away, he remarked one day to me thoughtfully, "Penney, your greatest work is yet to come." For some reason I didn't question him then as to his meaning. But, if I may say so without its seeming to be unbecoming, the opportunities that have been revealed to me in the last ten years or so, tied so intimately to the experiencing of God's power in my life and which Dr. Short so deeply wished for me, have made his remark seem often to me to have been prophetic.

In the summer of 1919 I married for the second time. My wife was highly educated, a lady possessed of a character of rare beauty, and of versatile talent.

To us was born a son, Kimball.

I had devoted my energies so unsparingly to business for so many years that I began to feel some effects. And it was a warning of a rather somber kind to me when I applied for new life insurance and learned, on the basis of the physical examination, that the insurance company up-rated me ten years, thus cutting in half the amount of insurance applied for.

I have never been a believer in allowing inferior situations to drift; for an incentive to more activity out of doors I found a small estate in Westchester, a house and fifteen acres at

White Plains, called Whitehaven, which I added to so I could have horses, some cattle, sheep, poultry, a drove of Berkshires. I have from boyhood understood the restorative powers of new-turned soil and the associations of man with four-footed animals.

The year 1921 also saw the beginning of what was to become a many-faceted concern with the state of Florida.

In 1912 I had visited Palm Beach, with one of my sons who was ailing. I thought a good deal at the time about the superb and curative climate, and of developments which could come in relation to it.

In 1921, thinking that a winter place in Florida would add to the resources at Whitehaven for renewal of body and mind, I bought a place on the east coast, at Belle Isle in Biscayne Bay, linked up with the Venetian Causeway, a stone's throw from Miami Beach, two miles from the mainland.

Besides the reasons connected with my health, and a base of recreation for my family, I had an unformed but insistent sense that there was an important future for that section of Florida.

The small-scale animal husbandry activities at Whitehaven directed my thinking more and more to matters of livestock and agriculture. I had, of course, been born to an interest in them. My father's love of fine horses and cattle had led me naturally as a young boy to share the ordinary chores, and care of animals. There had been my own never-to-be-forgotten pig venture.

Beyond these influences, too, as far back as the days of starting out in Kemmerer, I had perceived that, since stores in small towns are naturally dependent in great measure on rural people, prosperity for farmers means prosperity for our stores. Thus, in the broad sense, farmers' problems are our problems also.

By the onset of the twenties we had over three hundred stores, located in a large number of states, and my incessant trips among them enabled me to form a clear impression of agricultural conditions and problems. It seemed to me that nearly everywhere I went farmers stood in need of better cattle.

The low grade of beef and dairy animals in most sections of the country made me heartsick. Upon investigation I learned that the average butterfat production for the country was about 150 pounds per cow, and that only 3 per cent of the cattle were purebreds.

I was astonished and considerably distressed to learn further that every great purebred herd which had been built up in the United States had been dispersed upon the death of the owner, to settle his estate. The result was that nothing remained wherewith to carry on his work.

This was a contrast, and a disadvantageous one, I felt, to the situation in England and Scotland, for instance, where certain families have bred cattle for generations, with resultant opportunities for a degree of perfection in blood strains. In England a tradition of farming honor has grown up, and a pride in having blooded stock on a farm.

My study of the detailed situation in this country showed me, further, that the average life of a breeding unit here was less than ten years, and few had been in existence for as long as a quarter of a century.

Since the span of my lifetime at best must be too short a

period to work out the plan beginning to form in my mind, and wishing earnestly that posterity should carry on the benefits of any work I commenced, I decided, when I had assembled the components, that I would endow a herd of cattle.

I made the initial move by purchasing a farm where a great blood line could be laid down, with facilities for developing and carrying it on, under conditions which would make it self-perpetuating. In 1922 I acquired Emmadine Farm, a mile outside of Hopewell Junction in Dutchess County, New York, twelve miles from Beacon and Poughkeepsie. On Emmadine's 720 acres I set about laying the foundation of a practical, workaday institution for the improvement of pedigreed cattle and dissemination of tested scientific information to the farmers of the country.

Emmadine had been owned by Robert Stuart, who had equipped it at great expense in time and money as a modern dairy plant with several hundred dairy cows. Although I realize fully the importance of producing clean, wholesome milk, my plan was to make Emmadine a breeding rather than a dairy establishment. The water and the limestone foundation of the soil meant good bone, needed to breed good cattle.

After careful study I selected Guernseys, buying the best Guernsey brood cows I could find and four herd sires, among them Foremost 39191, and bracketing the name Foremost Guernsey Association and Emmadine Farm. Foremost had sold in 1916 for $3000.00; subsequently, to three Virginia dirt farmers, for $5000.00; and to me for $20,000.00. This price I decided was low for a sire of the qualities found upon investigation by Gordon Hall, whom I considered one of the best judges of cattle in the country.

I had in mind the application to this new venture of the fundamental principles which guided me in the foundation of the J. C. Penney Company. In agricultural and the pure-bred cattle business, as in any other, the honoring of ideals of hard work and golden-rule dealing with others would constitute a favorable climate in which to strive for the general good. For the guiding principle of Emmadine it was necessary to look no farther than the twelfth verse of the seventh chapter of the Gospel According to St. Matthew: "Therefore all things whatsoever ye would that men should do to you, do ye even so to them."

Seeking a man of principle and integrity as manager for Emmadine-Foremost Guernsey Association, I found him in Jimmy Dodge, who had been with C. I. Hood at his farm in Lowell, Massachusetts, for twenty years and was the leading figure in the art of selective breeding. Jimmy Dodge embodied the characteristics of men who labor to finest effect in the field of purebred stock. He was our friend, and it was a blow to us when he was killed in 1934 in an automobile accident. He was succeeded, with us, by William K. Hepburn, another among the ablest cattle judges and breeders in the United States. Such men are truly scientists; their work revolves around principles of agriculture, horticulture, biology, and animal husbandry, all of which require research, experimentation, continuous investigation. They are incurable optimists, possessed of indomitable determination and eagerness to share success with others. In this business there are no copyrights, exclusive patents, or trade secrets. The great

end toward which all bend their efforts is not simply the improvement of their own herds but the grading up of that
breed throughout the nation and the world.

To provide the framework for full and free development
of all we aspired to accomplish, for the benefit of whoever
could use our findings, wherever they might live, Emmadine
Farm-Foremost Guernsey was set up as a corporation, running till 1996, at which time its property is to be transferred
to the University of Missouri at Columbia, for the use of the
Department of Agriculture and the general propagation of
better cattle.

In a sense both Whitehaven and Emmadine represented
a form of home-coming for me. I had been long separated
from closeness to the soil. Not altogether realizing it, I had
harbored within me what can become the businessman's
homesickness for the good earth. Precedents are classic and
many for the human compulsion to relate oneself to the earth
after the peak of business struggle has been passed. When
Cato ceased to be a senator he turned to practicing agriculture.

Perhaps I can best indicate the ideal and hopes which
underlay the whole undertaking, and others set in motion by
it, if I tell an incident involving a man I met at the National
Guernsey Sale in Chicago in 1926, a person worthy of the
encouragement we wished, from the first, to emanate from
Emmadine.

August Johanik had been a boy of fifteen when his Polish
parents moved in 1909 from the coal regions of Pennsylvania
to a Slovak settlement in Wisconsin. There was a sort of
kinship between August and me; our families were poor,

and shared the same struggle to turn their land to productivity.

When August was eighteen events made him the head of the family. Within three years he had a nice little show herd. But then blackleg appeared in the herd. Nine head died. Yet August wouldn't be downed. A heifer, purchased at a price that meant crushing sacrifice, proved to be a runt, and he had no more than finished paying for it when it died.

Still, August Johanik didn't know how to quit.

After repeated failures he bought another purebred heifer (Mary's Pride of White Plains), which became the nucleus of his fine purebred herd. His bad luck was not all behind him yet, however. His barn and silo burned. Watching the angry flames he remarked simply, "Thank the Lord I've got enough insurance to start a new foundation!"

By this time he was deep in debt, and taxes were a burden. August knew times when the only food in the house was a loaf of bread, and there was sufficient money only to buy a sack of flour—or a bag of feed for the cows. The neighbors said he must be crazy to hang on. Even he could see how people might think that the only thing his purebreds would ever do for him would be to lead him to the poorhouse.

He entered his purebred cow in the National Guernsey Sale in mid-May, 1926, and that was where I met him. He was wrapped up in the hope that she might fetch $500.00, which would at least ease the load of his debts.

When she was knocked down it was for $2100.00, and I was the successful bidder. August could hardly believe it. I can well understand,—and it was not from any weakness in him,—why he went off by himself and cried when his beauty was sold. A lot of himself had gone into the quality of that creature.

The sale meant not only the easing of debt but freedom from it. It meant plenty of flour in the kitchen barrel, and feed in the bin. It meant shoes for the family, and overalls and percale dresses. But it meant much, much more. It meant the vindication of August Johanik's faith in what he and I both believe is a great calling.

I did him no favor in the price paid for the cow, because she was worth every penny of it. But the greatest part of the experience for me was seeing the encouragement August took from the incident. If, through Emmadine Farm, I could have a continuing part in helping men like August Johanik, and showing the way to better things on the American farm, it would be the best dividend I could receive on an investment.

New interests sometimes make a new man. It was an interesting by-product of my Whitehaven and Emmadine ventures, that the insurance companies re-examined me, removed the ten-year up-rating, and accepted my application for $2,000,000.00 in life insurance policies.

A year or so after I had acquired Emmadine, my wife passed on, leaving me with the son, Kimball—presently in the active reserve of the U. S. Navy—who is very like his mother. I had a fresh sense of loss but, too, of rich memories of a serene and gracious personality, and, through her, of a sense of discovery of many cultural treasures.

## CHAPTER ELEVEN

At the end of 1923 a matter arose which was of business interest to me and my associates but of special sentimental interest as well to me.

Mr. Sams had been President of the J. C. Penney Company six years, and Penney stores were in 475 communities.

We learned that the store of J. M. Hale & Brother in Hamilton, was for sale. I went at once to see Mr. Hale, who had given me my first drygoods store job, twenty-eight years earlier. I bought the store. It caused a little local flurry for of course it was an interesting outcome of events.

Mr. Hale remarked after we signed the papers, "You know, Jim, for quite a while I've been thinking it was rather odd that you opened stores in a great many places, yet didn't open one here in Hamilton. I'd have thought you'd especially want to be here, where your folks were, where you were born, where you got started in dry goods."

"Well, you see, Mr. Hale, up to now we just weren't ready for Hamilton."

"The boys around town are talking about Jim Penney buying out his first boss. Maybe you should have come in several years back, forced me to sell out to you instead of waiting for me to retire. Maybe that way it would have been a better deal for you."

"I'm satisfied, Mr. Hale. As I told you, we weren't ready up to now." We branched off to talking about other things.

I didn't disclose to Mr. Hale that he had touched on something which had been in my mind a long time. I had wanted to come into Hamilton, but to come in the way I'd want another man to come if it were my store which was there first. The only Hamilton location that would interest me was Mr. Hale's location; in my own mind I had decided, some years earlier, that there couldn't be any Penney store in Hamilton until Mr. Hale got ready to retire and take down his name.

It all worked out well, even to the nice round number of the store in the Penney chain. It was the 500th Penney store which opened on the spot where I learned, among many others, the valuable lesson that pretty much anyone can sell new stock, but it takes a real salesman to sell the tail ends, the last two of a dozen, in which is tied up the profit.

In 1923, at a dinner of the Committee of 1000 on Law Enforcement, called by Fred B. Smith of the YMCA Evangel to Men at the old Sherry's on Fifth Avenue, I met a man who made a striking impression on me.

The Committee of 1000 was not so concerned with prohibition, per se, as with observing the legality of the Eighteenth Amendment.

The man I encountered that evening was Dr. Daniel A. Poling, then pastor of the Marble Collegiate Church, at Fifth Avenue and 29th Street, New York City, and also leader of the International Christian Endeavor Society.

At the time I was giving much thought to what Dr. Short had impressed upon me as the obligation and privilege of

men of means to generously assist those forms of philanthropy
and humanitarian education which, in their very nature,
must be supported by contributions from private individuals.
I was mulling over some type of foundation and some needed
job which a foundation could do. I was of the opinion that I
preferred at least one aspect of it to benefit young people.
A carefully designed foundation could carry out a method
for which I had a taste: relating people to people, for the
working out of problems.

It has almost invariably turned out with me that the answer to a problem or venture came, not in the guise of an
academic plan or an elaborate blueprint, but in the form of
a man. That evening at Sherry's I gleaned enough about
some of Dr. Poling's ideas to prompt me to see him again
later. I had my partner Ralph Gwinn see him also. Several
years were to elapse before I found the concrete way to link
my sense of discovery in Dr. Poling and just the right form of
organization for service to young people with problems of
direction and human behavior to solve.

By early 1925 Emmadine Farm was well established.

Much misunderstanding existed as to the purposes of
stock improvement. Old-school farmers dismissed pedigreed
animals casually as "fancy stock," kept for show rather than
practical use. Although the acquisition of Emmadine had,
to some extent, grown indirectly out of my need for the re-
freshment of outdoor activity, it had rapidly become something quite other than an expensive fad or hobby. There
was new and constructive adventure in setting up a means of
a permanent contribution to the advancement of the dairy

industry, which was of basic importance to millions of people, among them communities in which our stores were located. It didn't surprise me greatly when some of our managers took up the idea, and the work, of introducing purebred stock into their home neighborhoods.

Emmadine suggested to me a whole new range of inquiry, into the application of science to agriculture. Especially, I began turning over in my mind the potential of applying to farm management the partnership idea which, in our company, had been such a powerful builder of men.

It could be said, as well of these interests as of the stores, that in the next few years I put *in the place of religion*—in the worshipful, churchgoing sense—the energy and enthusiasm of what I conceived to be my first duty, to my partners and the projects which engaged us.

I did not, in this period, practice positive Christian living, by praying as I should, attending church in a serious and worshipful frame of mind, and otherwise holding to a sense of closeness to a higher Power.

Born as I had been to the agricultural environment and its fundamentals, the activities into which I plunged at this juncture were rather more complex, I found, than those in which I had been grounded on my father's farm. Among the simplest differences was the fact that I had a great deal of money to work with. As time went on some rather bad mistakes grew out of that fact, not the smallest of which was the easy assumption that, merely with money, a man can do anything; even that no mistake can ever be so serious that it can't be corrected with money.

Spending a good part of the winters at Belle Isle I was rapidly becoming very Florida-minded. The real estate market in that period was like another New York Stock Exchange, roaring with ballooning values. Millionaries were being made overnight, in such numbers that the man who did not become a millionaire was the oddity, not the millionaire.

All my innate caution warned me against such an overblown phenomenon. I could see certain basic and permanent values in the picture as it related to Miami. I had an absolute conviction as to its future, a faith which I am happy now to remember never changed, even in the face of what others mistook for fatal setbacks.

Nevertheless, I vowed that, inevitable as I believed the brightness and stability of Miami's long-range future to be, I would abide by my own habits of doing business and not be drawn into the whirlpool churned up by hysterical apostles of the in-and-out dollar.

Wherefore, though I passed by the prevailing frenzy on the other side of the street, so to speak, I did feel impelled to buy some timberland. Timberland is in the primeval category, more elemental than real estate. Having bought it I would forget it, allow its value to appreciate.

A lifelong friend interested me in a tract of 120,000 acres in Clay County, on the west bank of the St. Johns River (sometimes called the American Nile), at the northern end of the central ridge section of the state. Of the tract 20,000 acres had been cleared. The company which had controlled it had abandoned an unsuccessful venture and the tract was in the hands of the court.

The cleared land appealed to me as offering a site for setting in motion a new kind of partnership project.

I acquired the whole tract in the name of the Penney-Gwinn Corporation, which was a new facet of my association with Ralph W. Gwinn, a lawyer who had helped us at the time our articles of incorporation were being adapted to our unique makeup and financial requirements. By a rather interesting lesson to us in the economics of legal advice, Mr. Gwinn had become the attorney for our company and remained so until he entered politics and became the Republican representative in Congress of the 27th New York district.

In the autumn of 1925 operations began at Penney Farms, eight miles west of Green Cove Springs, county seat and principal city of Clay County. We had a 100-mile network of roads, twenty-five miles of which were paved to a width of sixteen feet. There were 300 houses, 125 of them good substantial farmhouses.

I placed 3000 range cattle on the land, established an experimental poultry plant of 4000 purebred birds, provided for a dairy herd and a drove of purebred swine. An Institute of Applied Agriculture was set up, and central services were developed for the information and guidance of settlers.

All these experiments I undertook on my own initiative and at my private risk. There was no connection whatever between them and the J. C. Penney Company, save as they were reflections of my personal experience with the principles underlying the partner-manager plan, and the concept of partnership between the stores and the communities which our stores exist to serve.

At Penney Farms I had nothing to sell, in the ordinary

meaning of the term. I employed no salesmen, did no advertising. Farms were to be evolved and farmers trained in the best scientific practices of agriculture. My personal representative was D. Walter Morton, formerly dean of the Oregon School of Commerce.

When we had rehabilitated old farm buildings and made ready roads to render marketing of farm crops convenient, we turned to selection of future owners of the farms.

Conventionally, farms are sold to all comers who can pay for them. We carried on the selection of settlers through the 745 Penney stores. Families known and recommended by the managers of stores were put on a preferred list. I put in charge of the farm management F. O. Clarke, formerly head of the Vocational Department of Berea College, Berea, Kentucky. When a good number of farmer prospects had been located in a given area, Mr. Clarke got on a train and went to find out more about them, through personal interview and suitable inquiries in their communities. We felt that the right people would be workers, with a talent or persuasion for farming and the temperament to fit well into a co-operative community. As time went on we took some men who had never farmed a day in their lives but who harbored the farming impulse, desired to live in the country, and were willing to work.

The method of making each store manager a one-third owner in the store of which he had charge was applied at Penney Farms, except that in this situation the plan went a step farther. After a farmer had lived on his farm for one year he was given the opportunity of purchasing and owning it in full, if he felt satisfied to do so, and provided he had measured up to the standards of character and industry set up by me through the Penney Farms management.

From the outset I laid down the absolute rule that Penney Farms had no room in its plans for any man who used liquor or smoked cigarettes. Also, any man who came into the situation with us must be a regular churchgoer.

When we and a prospective farmer were satisfied that Penney Farms was the right project for him, no payment for the twenty-acre farm plot was required, then or during the first six months of occupancy. The farmer needed to have sufficient money to maintain himself and his family for the time needed to bring in his first crop and to insure the farmhouse when he took possession of it for $750.00.

The fact that if, at the end of the six months, the farmer and the corporation were mutually satisfied, it was then possible to arrange to buy the farm out of its profits within a specified time introduced the important incentive of ownership. And the experiment stations and other facilities gave the farmer access to divers advantages which a lone farmer could seldom if ever have.

The first year forty farmers came in, the second about fifty. The first year three of the forty withdrew. The wife of one was not able to feel contented, and the other two were not really looking for the underlying idea of Penney Farms.

The venture harmonized well with my interpretation of the golden rule, and the obligation I had to the fact that I got my start in the store business through the lift which the original owners of my first store gave me. Penney Farms became, in effect, my expression of the fact that, if Mr. Johnson and Mr. Callahan could have faith in me, they had laid it upon me to pass along that faith by reposing faith in other men. Through me, confidence in the ability of men to assume positions of responsibility when given a little encouragement and a share in the profits of labor, had built up our big and trusted force of store managers, and made our company what it was. In turn, the underlying principles and stability of our company had made Penney Farms possible too, another link in the chain of practicing the golden rule.

People said to me, "But aren't farmers different from store people—too individualistic to fit into a truly co-operative scheme?"

I never feel that farmers are a separate breed of human beings. Just like anyone else, farmers respond to a little encouragement, a clear-cut incentive. In establishing Penney-Gwinn Farms Mr. Gwinn and I figured out that there were a good many farmers in this country who were just getting by, or perhaps were falling just a little short of getting by. Perhaps they were farming too much land, or their soil was poor, or their mortgage was too heavy. Probably they would never be able to work out their salvation alone. When I could look at one of the farms and reflect that, for a single picking of beans, the woman who owned it had got over $175 one week, I knew that there was something good indeed in a plan of assistance to give worthy farmers a start.

One day I went to call on Dr. Poling again. He had impressed me as a militant defender of the younger generation, a born youth leader. For some time he had been interested in a Young People's Radio Conference, which featured an inspirational address based on the teachings of Jesus, followed by questions and answers about the problems of youth.

Dr. Poling had many interests and was by no means looking for a job, but I explained to him that I had decided to set up a J. C. Penney Foundation and asked him to be its Director. The company's building on 34th Street west of Eighth Avenue was nearing completion and I arranged to set aside offices for the foundation on the eighteenth floor. Dr. Poling agreed to come in with me on the foundation, on a part-time basis.

When he took up the directorship, January 1, 1926, he became leader of the National Youth Radio Conference, meeting several hundred young people each Sunday afternoon in one of the public rooms of the old Waldorf-Astoria. At first the meetings were broadcast on a single local station, but they soon became so influential that thirty-eight stations of the Blue Network of the National Broadcasting Company carried what had quickly come to be recognized as the outstanding youth guidance conference in the country.

As a corollary a vocational guidance program was set up within the foundation. Dr Poling brought in Leonard Miller from YMCA work in Philadelphia to direct that part of the expanding plan.

By venturing into the field of vocational guidance, through the National Youth Radio Conference, Dr. Poling fully realized from the first that he was undertaking a somewhat daring experiment. It called for exploration of new paths, the planning of new techniques, the widest and most exact contacts with existing social and educational agencies, in the nationally radio-reached area.

Mr. Sams became chairman of Dr. Poling's Radio Committee, made up of businessmen of national reputation. But as I have said, the J. C. Penney Foundation was a privately endowed activity, wholly separate from the J. C. Penney Company; therefore Mr. Sams served in a personal capacity rather than in any way as an officer of the company.

An idea came to me during the dark watches of one night which, if I could translate it into tangible form, might be a bright and shining lodestar throughout the lifetime of Penney Farms.

In the early morning I went into the room of my associate, Mr. Gwinn, and asked him what he would think of a home community of apartments and a church edifice "for all the saints, who from their labors rest. . . ," namely, retired ministers and their wives. He approved the idea as a memorial to my parents, and in so doing cheered and encouraged me.

My father had died in 1895, and my mother in 1913. It seemed to me that a chapel surrounded by homes for men and women who had devotedly followed the Christ whom my parents served, pouring out their lives for the holy cause in which my parents lived and died, would be fitting as an expression of my gratitude.

Accordingly, in June, 1926, ground was broken at Penney Farms for the Memorial Home Community, and the cornerstone laid for the Penney Memorial Chapel.

Shortly afterward I went abroad again. Dr. and Mrs. Poling were in London, and I had the benefit there of their friendly companionship.

During that summer, at Paris, I married the present Mrs.

Penney, the young woman of striking intelligence and even, sweet habit of mind who was to become the mother of my two daughters. Her sympathetic and generous disposition, the compatibility of our interests in people and world changes have made me a better, bigger person. The steadfastness and projection of her religious faith and its unquestioning depth have been an influence in the spiritual change I have experienced, and I feel blessed.

We have experienced unbounded joy in our daughters, Mary Frances, named for my mother, and Carol Marie, named for her mother and grandmother. We sometimes laugh in the family, saying that there is nothing like two young daughters to encourage a sense of humor in a father. More important even than that, however, each in her way has brought me in stimulating touch with things which young people are thinking and talking about. Mary Frances was graduated from Massachusetts Institute of Technology, going on to Oxford University for advanced study in chemistry. Carol Marie, a senior at Stanford University in the fall of 1950, chose political science as her field of specialization.

There have been many occasions when I regretted the limitations of my formal education. I have benefited from the girls' very diversity of interests; their independent viewpoints, (often in subjects for which I never had time as I was coming along,) have spurred me to make up for it as I was able, by continuing to study and learn.

Back again in the States, one day Dr. Poling and I were walking across town from my office, and I broached another subject to which I had been giving careful thought.

Dr. Poling was editor of *Christian Herald*. This publication, which I knew to be of important value to the Protestant denominations on a truly interdenominational basis, had gone through numerous vicissitudes. It had been my privilege to render some incidental assistance, but I had been thinking that its service could be strengthened, its range increased, by stabilizing it for the future, under Dr. Poling's continuing editorship.

"I have been thinking," I said, "that I might arrange to apply to *Christian Herald* and my further support of it the practical partnership principle that has built the stores to strength and stability. What would you think about it?"

And so it came about. *Christian Herald* came into the orbit of the J. C. Penney Foundation. I never dictated policies or procedure. It is always better to find someone qualified, and possessed of the enthusiasm to do a job, and then set him free to do it. Though the fuller development of *Christian Herald* was left absolutely under Dr. Poling's direction to those equipped by training to carry it on, it was a source of personal satisfaction that my means could assist what seemed to me a truly effective messenger of God's Word and work.

The week end beginning Friday, April 22, in 1927 represented for me a moment in time of tender memory. During those days, within the over-all framework of the J. C. Penney Foundation, we dedicated the memorials at Penney Farms to my parents.

The Home Community, a grouping of houses of Norman-Gothic influence, provided apartments for ninety-eight families. For each couple a quiet place of three rooms and bath, fully furnished and equipped for housekeeping, and for that delicate purpose, the rounding out of chapters in their lives' fulfillment.

Through the whole of a cool, sparkling Sunday the dedication of the chapel went on. Dr. Short was there with me to deliver the dedicatory sermon. It touched me that Mr. Gwinn had chosen to give the chapel a beautiful organ, as a memorial to his own mother. She had been a lover of music, and her home had been a stopping place on their long journeys for the circuit riders of the West; it seemed altogether fitting that her life should be memorialized in company with the lives of my own parents.

My two elder sons were donors of a memorial to their mother, Berta Hess Penney, in the form of a lovely screen, leading from the chapel into the community rooms, the door of the screen bearing her name in letters of gold.

Thus, together with the acquisition of Emmadine Farm, and the establishment of Penney Farms with its varied aspects, it seemed to me that I was entering on rich new privileges in passing on to my fellow-man what early home influences and the faith in me of men like Mr. Hale, Mr. Johnson, and Mr. Callahan had collectively inspired me to achieve.

# CHAPTER TWELVE

Some experiences in the Miami area of Florida marked the sort of milestone which tries a man's soul. But I am grateful to God that, more vividly than the human disillusionment and distress, the passing of time has enabled me to remember, rather, the blazing glory of sunsets over Biscayne Bay. Those sunsets seemed to me like a "Well done!" from Nature for the faith and vision of men who transformed a mangrove swamp into one of the most creatively beautiful reclamations of land ever known.

In the twenties my earlier acquaintance with south Florida as a vacation spot led to the serious interest in north Florida as well, where I named the large Clay County tract Penney Farms and on it developed the farm project and founded the Memorial Home Community and chapel in memory of my parents.

The more I became acquainted with them the more the possibilities of the state as a whole fascinated me, though I concentrated my own activity in the rural area of the north and the Miami area of the east coast.

My confidence was not disturbed by the damage done the east coast by the tropical hurricane which whipped in from the ocean in mid-September of 1925, wreaking a havoc of wind and water. Nor did the economic setback and the collapse of the boom dampen my zest.

Of course a conservative such as myself would instinctively be wary after the awful speculative losses which marked the collapse of the boom. But I had faith in the restorative powers of time and the farsighted practicality of such men as Carl Fisher, Dr. John G. Dupuis, R. B. Polk, the Tatums, and other leaders.

Carl Fisher had earlier conceived and demonstrated the conviction that Indianapolis was the ideal place for the largest automobile speedway in the world. In 1913 he visited Florida for reasons of health. He was so inspired by its natural endowments that he remained, applying the same quality of vision and genius for planning which had benefited Indianapolis to planning a city which was to make synonymous the names *Miami Beach* and *Carl Fisher*.

Dr. Dupuis, a physician and surgeon, used his scientific training in the interrelation of diet and health to develop fine dairy cattle, working with a pioneer's approach to control and safeguard health in a fast-growing area.

Mr. Polk, with his father a leading figure in the canning industry, had worked with the United States Army on food supply in World War I and applied himself to developing new and improved canning machines and methods, with particular relation to grapefruit production in south Florida.

Others joined them, drawing on a wide variety of business experience to participate in development of an area which they sensed had tremendous potential importance.

In my own mind there was no question whatever that an area so richly blessed by Nature as to location, climate, and accessibility to three-quarters of the population of the country, would recover its equilibrium and come eventually into its own.

As I saw it in 1926 and 1927, what Miami needed most was *friends,* who believed not only in her future but that she *had* a future, and who would act accordingly.

In that spirit I went into the City National Bank of Miami, first as a substantial stockholder, subsequently as chairman of the board. The bank needed help, and I had the desire to render it.

There is no desire on my part to profess anything unearthly in this action. Although I would not deny that the atmosphere was captivating—constituting a moment for action in which literally everything smelled of money—nevertheless my impulse was to help out in a distressed bank situation, not simply to make money.

My entire business career had conditioned me against succumbing to the lure of huge profits made overnight. The strengthening of the bank seemed to me part of an over-all, long-range development of the area it served. I had never been a stock-market speculator and was free by both temperament and experience from the plunging, helter-skelter impulses characteristic of the idea that quick-moving situations will surely make quick money for people who enter them.

In addition to my interest in the bank, I became a substantial participant in a real-estate development known as Miami Shores. On all sides soaring prices were being made, so to speak, a virtue. Miami Shores attracted me because it was development policy to hold prices to conservative levels. That agreed with my fixed belief that no buying is justified except it be related to basic values. That is now, and always has been, the uncompromising premise of the Penney stores.

I went into the real-estate enterprise, therefore, on the basis of my considered judgment that development of the southeastern shoreland was a positive need, a logical next step.

In direct relation to the Miami area it had been demonstrated that back-country farms could now satisfactorily supply the estimated urban markets, of which Miami Shores was a part. The development of one was nurtured by the development of the other.

I envisioned the advantages of Florida and the Miami area as more and more appealing to people who lived in the thickly populated sections of the country, especially those east of the Rockies. I was familiar with these people and their ways and felt I wanted to have a helping hand in shaping advantages in Florida which would have a vacationing or permanent appeal for them.

I was still, of course, primarily concerned with the growth of the J. C. Penney Company. The City National Bank of Miami was one of several enterprises which absorbed my thought and action at this juncture, yet I must admit it was a special challenge to me. I saw it as a vital cog in a new and eminently constructive activity. It was a matter of grave responsibility to me, and some understandable pride of reputation, that my connection with the City National Bank attracted to it many depositors.

Meanwhile, in New York, the activities of the J. C. Penney Foundation were expanding. Borrowing for the purpose from five banks, using my personal holdings of shares in the

J. C. Penney Company for collateral, I poured formidable sums into the Foundation.

As all the world knows, the black period 1929-1932 intervened. No geographical areas, however favored by Nature, and few individuals, however financially strong, were spared.

Once more Florida and everybody in it was badly hurt.

As the depression deepened, from time to time some commercial loans in the bank portfolio became unsatisfactory to the examiners. None of them was connected in any way with me personally, or with J. C. Penney Company or the Penney-Gwinn Corporation. Several times I took over slow or unacceptable loans, substituting cash; it amounted to hundreds of thousands of dollars. I continued borrowing on my personal stockholdings to do it. My confidence in my own financial invulnerability was complete. I borrowed more millions to put into the needs of *Christian Herald,* Memorial Home Community, Penney Farms, National Youth Radio Conference, Emmadine Farm, and Foremost Dairy Products, Inc.

Stock prices in general began a strange, downward plunge. Banks called their loans. The panic lasted not days but years.

A thousand reasons were advanced to explain it. Many of us were prompted, no doubt, more by frantic anxiety to stave off recognizing the disaster for what it was than by willingness to face the truth and gain a real comprehension of forces involved.

Occasional brief rallies of prices touched off false hopes that there was no involvement which was fundamental. But as months wore on, declines in stock values reached

$15,000,000,000, a sum so gigantic in those days as to seem hard to put into everyday language. Before 1931 it was to reach $50,000,000,000.

The more serious the general financial situation became, the more I pledged my personal holdings to borrow large amounts of cash, to keep the bank sound, and to support the other projects which were feeling the distress of the times. In the time that I was in the bank I put in a cash total of $1,800,000, which I lost. The Penney-Gwinn Corporation loaned the bank over $2,334,000, which it lost. In the end my debts exceeded $7,000,000, all incurred to save what to me were public-spirited enterprises.

Finally my credit was exhausted and I could no longer borrow. To my distress I had to cease the gifts to philanthropic and development activities which I had been privileged to make.

When it was no longer possible to go farther with my support of *Christian Herald,* I called on Dr. Poling. "I have made up my mind to just give the property to you, no strings attached," I explained. "I feel well satisfied to leave it completely in your hands. Now you must go forward with it."

At about the same time I terminated the agricultural project at Penney Farms which was publicly identified with me. Morally it had been a voluntary undertaking, and I was under no legal obligation to continue it.

I have always felt that the vast farm project was worth while in the attempt. We set up a new plan of farm ownership, which appeared to offer sound opportunities for farmers, and others with a feeling for the soil, who wanted to own, and live by, the land.

*By way of a hard awakening we did, however, learn some*

*valuable lessons. Of them all undoubtedly the most valuable
was that, of itself, money will not insure the success of any
project or any life. It is possible to possess material wealth
and yet to be a failure.*

At Penney Farms, as we found out through bitter experience, we went at things too fast, without effective preparation—a mistake which is not uncommon when men rely too
confidently on the authority of money. Too often money
destroys the sense of humility, of being willing to learn
from the experience of others.

For example, we took no time to learn from those who
knew best what the soil of Clay County was capable of. Even
the experts on soil whom we employed overlooked fundamental knowledge under the magic spell of money. In the
rush to make the soil produce we imported plants and fruits
wholly unsuited to either soil or climate. Nor did we use a
wise method in picking the people to work on the land of
the new settlement. Some came because they believed the
settlement would need stores, and they wanted to learn storekeeping rather than to farm. Many had the impression that
hard work would not be needed, because there was money
behind the project. Others were dependent-minded, rather
than rugged independents, which the farms were designed to
build. Like ourselves, many were too undisciplined, too unprepared by learning as to elements involved, to withstand
the demands of a new environment. No amount of money
can pay the price of lack of discipline and preparation.

The failure was my fault, for I put on people a burden
of responsibility which was too much for them, as indeed it
was for me.

It was a severe lesson to me, in the fact that the practice of the golden rule requires more than money and a disposition of good will toward one's neighbors.

After the resettlement project was discontinued, the property was sold to a subsidiary of Foremost Dairies, Inc. Profiting by experience, that company rediscovered the truth that Nature is the best teacher. The Clay County tract had grown slash pine for centuries, a crop that enriched the South originally. So now the new company has a beautiful and profitable reforestation project, and trees are its leading inhabitants. Next to trees are range cattle, of strains which improve on those that have come down from the Spanish who settled the land 300 years ago.

In spite of all that could be done to hold the line, the City National Bank was forced to close its doors, and did so December 24, 1930.

That banks could fail in a city of fabulous values and promise; that a free economic system—which had enabled me with my partners to build a company such as the J. C. Penney Company, whose foundation seemed to me so solid as to be everlasting—could see values wither away like parched grass, was a new experience, new knowledge for me. That my moral responsibility and personal character could be attacked— these events brought me to the brink of a real unknown.

Never before, to my knowledge, had the honor of any dealings of mine been questioned. It was a cherished reputation. Now, in a matter of hours, I was confronted by conditions and accusations which I could never have imagined. Among the smaller distresses a sorry gibe gained currency that I had even manufactured a middle name—*Cash*—to attract attention to my cash-and-carry stores. As a great many people were well aware, the full name of my father, a Baptist preacher who ironically enough never got any cash at all for preaching, was James Cash Penney.

It is not constructive here to resurrect the details of chaotic happenings resulting from the Miami collapse. But it is relevant to say that the jolting shock made me realize the extent to which, in the complexity of events, I had permitted the idea of the power of money to possess me.

When I worked for $6.00 a week at Joslin's Dry Goods Store back in Denver, it was my ambition, in the sense of wealth in money, to be worth $100,000.00 some day. When I reached that goal I felt a certain temporary satisfaction, but it soon wore off and my sights were set on becoming worth a million dollars.

As time went on I became big in my own mind, increasingly confident that means bring invulnerability.

The result of that type of thinking was inevitable. Coasting along comfortably on my inherited spiritual capital, when catastrophe engulfed me I hardly knew which way to turn. What I had allowed to become my main dependence was not there to sustain me.

In my heart and mind I knew I had done no moral wrong. Practical people know that no man's resources will be unlimited forever. Relatively few people really believed that, if I would, I could have saved the bank.

Nevertheless, I was keenly affected by the fact that people had suffered financial loss in a situation where I had of my own free will made myself heavily responsible. Notwithstanding the inexorable fact that, being no exception, my capital was hypothecated by the general drop in all stock values, the outcome went crushingly against my innate habits of mind and the consistent record of my entire business history.

For every dollar anyone had ever spent with the J. C. Penney Company he had received maximum exchange in value and service. Compared with the fact that depositors of a bank in which I was an officer had actually lost money, there was a terrible insignificance to the money I had lost by pouring it into the bank in a sincere effort to stabilize it through a period of external formative influences.

In the purely personal sense it was part of the whole shocking episode that three of the five banks from which I had borrowed large sums called my loans. Legally it was their right, but it struck a severe blow at my feeling of personal integrity.

A man must regard very soberly indeed the unheralded fact of being literally forced to start over again at the age of fifty-eight to provide for his family.

Two of the banks having rejected their right to close me out, a portion of my stock was thereby saved, providing a certain basis for financial recovery.

Inevitably it was a slow process. Years of grueling mental agony ran their plodding course while legal aspects of the over-all situation were fought through the courts.

Constantly throughout the days in court I carried a slip of paper in my pocket, on which I had copied down Psalms 91:4—"He shall cover thee with His feathers, and under His wings shalt thou trust. His truth shall be thy shield and buckler." As I went over and over these words in my mind, I could not help but think, with penitent sadness, what my father would say, knowing that I had allowed myself under any circumstances to reach such extremity before finding the time, and the room in my harried mind, to think more about the power of God and less about the power of money.

When my father was excommunicated he counseled me repeatedly not to feel bitter toward the people who drove him and my mother from the Primitive Baptist Church which they loved. In my own Gethsemane I wished to be as forbearing as he; yet so unjustified was the accusation that I ran out on the bank, that for a long time I wrestled hopelessly with the urge to rebellion and bitterness.

There were many inner obstacles to conquer. It took much time, and an entirely new kind of discipline, for my thinking to clarify to the point where I could ponder that it was not Jesus' way to fritter away time and strength straining for personal vindication. It was sufficient, for Him, to occupy His time with returning good for evil.

I was flat broke, touching bottom.

Mrs. Penney and I continued to live at Whitehaven, hoping to work things out. We let the servants go, and the outside men on the place, and in the Spring of '32 closed off all but two rooms in the house. One has a strange feeling, continuing to be close to a house which, having seen much living, has become dark and empty. While we lived in the two rooms, Mrs. Penney did the housework. Whitehaven was the only home we had. Would we be able to save that much from the ruin of my affairs?

Suicide is not in my nature, or retreat. Though the burden

was immense the only thing possible was to find the way back to solid ground.

When disaster came we had already begun preparing a new section of pastureland at Whitehaven.

It is amazing how quickly land will return to wilderness if it finds the chance. In my spare time, with one pair of hands, I could hardly make much impression at what the ten men it had been necessary to call off the work had been doing. But working with soil and stone can be quieting in time of personal crisis and, to occupy myself, I began spending most of my spare time working on this piece of pastureland.

Nerves played strange tricks on me sometimes while I pulled weeds and cleared off stones. Straightening up for a moment to ease sore muscles, I would imagine that any minute someone would be coming to serve me with new papers in some proceeding.

I soon saw that it would be more constructive to begin going back over my experience, taking stock of assets remaining within myself. Had anything which had happened changed the faculties and character of the inward person I was when my father concluded, "Jim will make it"? No. No one had robbed me of the will and know-how to work hard and serve the public. That was the fundamental equipment which had started me off in Kemmerer, on the cumulative merchant experience which had made the Kemmerer store the mother of a large family of stores.

When events combine to bring a man to financial ruin and the road ahead seems blocked, what does he do?

Slowly my thinking cleared to the degree that made answers begin to come.

First of all, I reminded myself, a man doesn't run. Neither does he squander time and strength in blaming everything and everyone in sight—excepting himself. When he has brought himself around to accepting the fact that possessing money will never be a guarantee of invulnerability and that whatever fortune he had has been lost, the way is opened to seeing that the only place left to go is—up. Powers remain,— the powers used to build with, in the first place.

And so he fights.

I never think back to this hard experience, and the lean days at Whitehaven, without recalling gossip which gained circulation and was given by the circumstances a certain rather wry humor. It was said that J. C. Penney personally received an income of $1.00 per day from each store in the J. C. Penney Company chain. In our circumstances, reduced to actual poverty, it would have been rather a helpful thing— had it been true!

I still encounter people who believe I'm retired from business and have ceased all connection with the company bearing my name. The fact is, I'm in my office at the Penney Company building every day I'm in New York. In the course of a year I probably visit more of our stores personally than the majority of officers of the company. To visit every store in the chain would take me five years, excepting Sundays and holidays.

The experiences of the early thirties brought me to the conclusion that a man will be a failure in life if he can be known for nothing but his wealth. We live in what is generally acknowledged to be a materialistic age; yet I see many signs that people do care more about what a man does to serve his times than about his wealth in dollars.

When I accepted the fact that disastrous events had not destroyed any essential capacities of mine, I began to fight. Fighting kept me going on, and going on kept me fighting.

It wasn't either quick or easy. When I got back on firm ground I had much less, in the material sense, than I had had. But the way opened for a fundamental change in me, and the discovery that God had plans for me other than just making money. With far less money than before, I was to find a peace of mind and happiness I had never known.

One morning a small incident, the significance of which could only be comprehended by myself, made me feel that at least I had made a beginning.

Walking from my home to the office I always passed an uptown branch of one of the banks which I felt had used me particularly badly. Out of resentment I made a practice for years of crossing the street in order to avoid passing close to the bank. One morning God put it into my heart to see that such petty resentment stood only in my own light. I decided to have done with it.

A bank guard was standing on the step, taking in the bright freshness of the morning sun. As I came up to him I said spontaneously, "Lovely day, isn't it?"

He smiled responsively. "Yes sir, it is a lovely day—beautiful."

For the first time in years I found myself feeling better about a number of things.

In that same connection, in February, 1950, I made a point of visiting Miami for the first time in twenty years.

God had helped me to rid myself of the last vestiges of bitterness. And I could only rub my eyes in amazement at present-day Miami. Everything I had thought about its potential, and more—as a residential paradise, a great port, a main terminal on the skyways—had come to pass. It gave me a feeling of satisfaction to know that my original judgment is upheld.

But more important to me was the feeling of gratitude to God for His power, through which I could see it all without resentment over reminders of the past.

# CHAPTER THIRTEEN

During a store visitation in the early thirties I had an engagement to speak at a noon luncheon in Battle Creek.

It was an effort to keep my engagement. I was feeling very ill, weighed down with pain and—though I did not comprehend it at the time—wrong thinking; I was convinced that the situation growing out of the Florida collapse had turned my friends, even my family—wife and children—against me. I was beset with nerves and able to sleep at all only by propping myself on one elbow.

At the luncheon I met an old friend, Dr. Elmer Eggleston, with whom I had gone to high school in Hamilton. He was a staff doctor at the Kellogg Sanitarium. I could see that he realized all was not well with me, and I felt so ill anyway that, as long as I was in Battle Creek, I asked him to go over me, to see what could be done.

My whole right side had broken out with an aggravated case of shingles, but I hadn't attributed what I took for "nerves" to a culmination of a long series of emotional and material shocks. Dr. Eggleston said I must break my trip immediately, and ordered me to bed in the sanitarium, assigning day and night nurses to the case.

That in itself filled me with panic. The plain fact was I

didn't have money to pay for such care. Yet I knew it would be useless to tell that to the doctor, who had known me for a long time as a man of wealth and would not be inclined to believe me even if I could subdue my pride sufficiently to tell him about my state of affairs.

For the time being the whole thing was taken out of my mind, however—after a fashion—by the prescribing by Dr. Eggleston of rather strong sedatives, to give me a chance to sleep and rest. All my life I have had an instinctive aversion to sedatives as well as stimulants, but now I felt so completely overwhelmed by the succession of shocks that I almost welcomed the merciful chance of escape into oblivion for a while.

After the surface of the exhaustion was somewhat rubbed down by the induced sleep I began to worry again, both about getting away from sedatives and about the bills for day and night nursing care.

One day the doctor said reluctantly, "Jim, if you'll promise me solemnly to follow instructions, we'll see if we can get along without the night nurse."

I felt tremendously relieved and, after taking the sedative he still insisted on, went to sleep about nine o'clock.

There was something else. The thought was strangely and clearly in my mind that I was coming to the end of my life, that by morning it would be over. I had the oddest feeling of being within myself, yet standing a bit to one side, watching the approaching end of living for me.

But at ten I waked up again. The doctor had said that if this happened I was to take another draught of sedative. Yet that seemed useless to me, when the other one had supplied barely an hour's sleep.

Things I wanted to say to my wife and children rushed into my mind, and I got out of bed, turned on the light, and wrote several letters. At last they were done. I sealed them, turned out the light, and returned to bed thinking I would sleep now, never doubting that when morning came I would no longer be alive.

But in the morning I was alive. To awake again was a strange kind of surprise. In some vague way I knew there must be a reason. What that reason could be I had no idea, nor did there seem any value in straining to puzzle it out.

I felt restless and apprehensive. It was still too early for the day nurse to come on duty. In order to do something, anything, I got up, put on my clothes, and wandered downstairs, thinking I would get some breakfast. But when I reached the mezzanine the dining room hadn't yet opened.

I felt as though an immense aloneness closed me in. I stood there, uncertain, in an emptiness that seemed to me to have no horizon.

Stealing softly along a corridor I heard the thread of an old, familiar hymn:

> Be not dismayed whate'er betide.
> God will take care of you. . . .

It seemed to be coming from a part of the building which contained the chapel. Seemingly without volition I moved slowly toward the sound.

The music grew clearer, the words distinct—

> All you may need, He will provide
> God will take care of you. . . .
> Lonely and sad, from friends apart. . .
> No matter what may be the test. . .
> God will take care of you.

I entered the chapel, sank down into a seat at the back.

> Lean, weary one, upon His breast,
> God will take care of you.

Quietly someone read a passage from Scripture. "Come unto me, all ye that are heavy laden, and I will give you rest. . . . Take my yoke upon you, and learn of me; for I am meek and lowly in heart, and ye shall find rest in your souls. For my yoke is easy and my burden is light. . . ."

The prayer followed.

Within myself, spontaneously, I groaned, "Lord, I can do nothing. Will you take care of me?"

In the next few moments something happened to me. I have never been able to explain it clearly in words and cannot now. I believe it was a miracle.

I had a feeling of being lifted, out of an immensity of dark space into a spaciousness of warm and brilliant sunlight. The thought flashed through my wearied mind that, if I had held myself responsible for such success as I had achieved, so too was I, and I alone, responsible for all the trouble that had descended upon me. But the great thing was that now I knew; God with His boundless and matchlessly patient love was there to help me. God had answered me when I cried out, "Lord, I can do nothing. Will you take care of me?" This was His answer.

A weight lifted from my spirit. I came out of that room a different man, renewed. I had gone in bowed with a paralysis of spirit, utterly adrift. I came forth with a soaring sense of release, from a bondage of gathering death to a pulse of hopeful living. I had glimpsed God.

As I thought of it in the days that followed, that strange,

vivid premonition I had had of death there alone in the night was in reality the death of the man I had been—made sick and despairing by wrong thinking—clearing the way for the birth within me of a new man. For the first time in my mature life I felt conscious of having touched His garment, and a dawning sense of rebirth, recapturing a vision of the faith of my parents. The good of the crises through which I had passed might appear slowly; but I could no longer doubt its final outcome.

I had breakfast, went back to my room. Throughout treatment and a bath I thought to myself, All my life I have been headstrong. I fought, because I thought that was the way to accomplish things I wanted to do. Here in this sanitarium I have been fighting the doctor, who wished only to make me well. Wrong thinking is my real illness. When I change my wrong thinking I shall be cured. My task is to become free within myself, with God's help, to follow His way.

I had badgered the doctor about being permitted to leave the hospital. Day by day he had put me off. "Well, we'll see—"

A convention trip had been laid out for me; the store managers were expecting me to meet them. I didn't realize at the time that Mr. Sams had been in daily communication with the sanitarium, and that the doctor's reports had led him not to expect me to participate in the convention. And, but for the turning point reached in the early morning at that quiet chapel service, the doctor would have refused to permit me to leave.

But, as a result of the change in me, part of which showed itself physically quite soon, the doctor changed from "Well,

we'll see—" (certainly a form of saying "Permission refused")
to "Well now, if you keep up this improvement—"

They were still reluctant to have me go to the convention.
But finally they agreed to allow it, at least for the first meeting, which was at Louisville.

At Louisville strength as I needed it was given to me.
Truly God was taking care of me. I went on to the next engagement, and the next.

Two weeks after that morning when I was drawn to the
sanitarium chapel by the strains of "God will take care of
you" I was back home, spending Christmas with my family.

In the next few months I gave much thought to taking
stock of myself. I sought to clear my clouded vision. I owed
some things to myself. The most important was giving Christ
a positive place in my life, my everyday affairs.

I had a returning courage and resolution as assets with
which to start over. I was not unaware that the way back
would yet be long, have many turnings. I had behind me
many years of being a very hardheaded man, never one to
*rely*. There was a great deal to undo.

Yet God had blessed me far beyond my deserts, notwithstanding fortuitous events which had resulted so critically
for me. Success had crowned our business because we had
been conscientious in practicing the golden rule all along
the line.

In other ways I had not followed Christ's teachings as I
should and might have, had not loved God as I should. I had
long carelessly neglected my obligations to His church, had

certainly been indifferent to working for the brotherhood of man as He had the right to expect a good follower to work.

Words in the sixteenth chapter of Matthew began having intimate deeper meaning for me: "For what is a man profited, if he shall gain the whole world, and lose his own soul? Or what shall a man give in exchange for his soul?"

From the days in Kemmerer and being on my own, I had allowed myself a steadily mounting conviction of my own adequacy. I was beginning to discover now how inadequate in His eyes I must be. How far I had drifted from the simple meanings of life, through growing big in my own mind!

In order to consolidate the glimpse of God's goodness and purpose in releasing me from the burdens which I had all but allowed to destroy me, back there at Battle Creek, I knew I must learn, specifically, to give myself over to God's plan for me. For now I was beginning to see that, patiently throughout the years of my preoccupation with business and success and the power of money, God had set in motion means of guiding, restraining influence on my life. I had been given both talents and experience as part of a plan.

As time went on and physical recovery progressed, I came to perceive that knowing God's will is not easy. One must seek it through prayer, with humility. The temptation is to strain our prayers through our own selfish and little desires, coloring our prayers with the hues of our own wills.

The core of prayer, namely, humility, became the core of my problem in picking up the parts of my business interests which, separate from the J. C. Penney Company, had fallen into such confusion. As I went about the obligations of restoring order to my all-round affairs, it was most necessary for me to learn the anatomy of true humility and, with God's help, to try to practice it.

Much was demanded of me immediately, in the way of living my new understanding, because I entered into what became the long and wearing court siege in which I faced a dogged determination from some quarters to prove deliberate wrongdoing on my part. Knowing what, to the best of my conscientious belief, had been in my mind throughout the whole episode, I found it a hard experience to sit day after day listening to attacks on my character and motives. But as events moved along I began finding that, if we will let Him, God provides strength as we need it.

My perspective both cleared and changed. Whereas I had experienced a heady elation in possessing substantial means, which I channeled to the assistance of a range of activities (from the advancement of purebred cattle to departments of religious and vocational interest embodied in *Christian Herald,* the National Youth Radio Conference, the Memorial Community, and so on), I began to perceive why the satisfaction of giving mere means eventually loses its savor. Dr. Short had schooled me in a philosophy of giving which was important and valuable. But of and by itself I began to comprehend that it was not enough.

As I examined my past it seemed contradictory that, whereas my partnership with men in the J. C. Penney Company had been much more than a mere money alliance, partaking equally if indeed not predominantly of spiritual and ethical bonds, my partnership with God hitherto, such as it was, had been expressed pretty much in terms of merely supporting His cause with money.

In a slow, faltering way I began to comprehend that giving of one's means is easy. Too easy, and therefore not nearly enough. Until a man can learn how to give of himself, he will not be giving after the example of the Saviour.

Not long after the strange and wonderful experience in Battle Creek a Texas minister, Dr. Frank Norris, pastor of the Fort Worth Baptist Church, wired me to see if I would speak on his radio broadcast. I agreed, and on the way south wrote out the notes for a talk which I felt I could make acceptably.

When I got to Fort Worth I noticed from the Sunday paper that I was announced "to take part in the church service at the First Baptist Church." Having agreed, so far as I knew, only to make a talk on the radio, I protested at once.

"Oh, but it won't do at all for you to let me down," Dr. Norris exclaimed. "I've advertised that you will be here and participate; many people will be greatly disappointed if you decline."

Seats had been reserved for my party of three or four and myself, well down at the front. I was uncomfortable about the idea of participating in the service and disinclined to accede. The service was held in a tent, to accommodate an audience of four or five thousand people.

I began to pay attention to the singing, which was perhaps as fine as any I had ever heard, and led by a choir of about a hundred. After one hymn Dr. Norris stepped to the edge of the platform and singled out someone in the audience. "Brother," he called, "I want you to come on up here, and help put the whoop in our singing."

That word *whoop* made me sit up immediately. I had been raised on my own father's "whoop" singing. Some readers may recall the popularity and emotional enthusiasm stirred by that type of religious singing, well known in the pioneer regions. It brought back such a flood of memory, reminding me too that I should be more ready to forget self, that I sent a note up to Dr. Norris: "If you still want me to talk, I'll be glad to—"

I told that great audience the simple story of my father and mother, and my own early religious training. Later, when Dr. Norris and I went to the broadcasting station, and I made ready to read my prepared talk, Dr. Norris exclaimed heartily, "Now look here, Brother Penney, just you tuck that paper back in your pocket for some other time. You tell the folks on the radio now the story you told earlier to the folks at the tent meeting!"

I did so, and marveled at the sense of strength which came to me from having put aside my own will.

I felt very strongly against letting the J. C. Penney Foundation go out of existence, even though resources for carrying on its various interests were diminished to almost nothing.

In its extremely curtailed form it was administering Emmadine, in Dutchess County, New York. Also, at the time I gave *Christian Herald* lock, stock, and barrel into Dr. Poling's keeping we had, for reasons of retrenchment, moved the Foundation offices from the J. C. Penney Building to *Christian Herald* offices on Fourth Avenue. By 1933, through Dr. Poling's wonderful administrative capacity and ability to attract such further financial assistance as was needed to carry *Christian Herald* over the hump, it was in the black, and beginning a steady climb to security and expanded service.

The charities which had functioned under the Foundation were reorganized and placed under the administration of *Christian Herald:* the Bowery Mission in New York; Montlawn, vacation center for underprivileged children near Nyack, New York; and the Industrial School and orphanages in Foochow, China.

For lack of continuously adequate capital the community buildings at Penney Farms had deteriorated; it was difficult to attract outside contributions to carry on the community because it had become so definitely identified as "a J. C. Penney interest" and no one saw any particular need to assist.

Dr. Poling, as indeed he has so often done in our long association, came up with an excellent and workable solution.

"The thing that should be done," he reflected, "is to give Memorial Home Community to *Christian Herald,* so we can then make it one, administratively, with Bowery Mission, Montlawn, and Foochow, a symmetrical quartet of *Christian Herald* interests, for children, retired ministers and wives, overseas missions, and rescue mission."

I thought it over for some time, to be sure it was the *best* solution. As a result—without strings, as in the case of *Christian Herald*—I turned over the Memorial Home Community to *Christian Herald.* Although I had resigned from the presidency of *Christian Herald* and eventually from the board, I continued on the board for the Memorial Home Community, because of my close personal involvement with the objective, as a living memorial to my parents.

It became a great satisfaction to me to see the J. C. Penney Community once again, under an altered administrative pattern, restored as a going concern, in the hands of the best people available for the creative vision and work involved.

Back in the twenties I had bought my father's old farm outside of Hamilton, Missouri. Before I got around to shaping it to a productive usefulness which I could feel would complement the work of Emmadine, distracting events intervened. But as I settled down along in the thirties to what would unquestionably be long-drawn-out legal proceedings, I began giving my mind more and more to a constructive realignment of business interests; and I felt very definitely that no activity was more constructive, inherently, than agriculture and livestock, reaching as it does into the daily life of us all; and that beginnings made at Emmadine could be diversified in other areas, under other agricultural conditions.

In the course of time I acquired six other farm tracts in Missouri in addition to the Home Place, all within a radius of a few miles from it.

Purebred Aberdeen-Anguses, Herefords, Pre-Eminent Guernseys, Suffolk and Corriedale ewes bred to Hampshire rams, and purebred hogs were our selected stock for the farms. And in selecting the managers for the farms the same qualities of integrity and principle, and the elements of the partnership idea carried out in the stores were the standard of judgment.

I was anxious that no one should get the impression that my expanding agricultural interests were a hobby. They were a business and must not only "stand on their own feet" financially but make money for my partners and me. Any sensible man intends and expects that his investments and work will make money for him. Nevertheless, money for its own sake was not my primary objective with the farms. I wanted what we did, first of all, to benefit others. If, through our efforts, our fellow-men should be able to have better animals with which to work, our ideal would be realized. I should say that my chief challenge to undertake the breeding of pure-bred cattle was the creative one of producing better livestock. And experience teaches me that it is creative, in the highest sense of the term, accomplishing results which will be both permanent and beneficial. To me, too, agriculture is not without an aspect of religion. On this point people have sometimes taken issue with me; but I explain my conviction by pointing out that in religion, as in agriculture, the ideal is *improvement*. As I grow older it seems to me that the same striving for improvement and usefulness which are part and parcel of religion is to be found in the earnest practice of agriculture and animal husbandry.

The encouragements to stick to my agricultural interests year after year have been many, in spite of incidental obstacles. The most important encouragement, undoubtedly, is that a solid foundation of accomplishment has been laid. High-grade cattle of the Guernsey, Aberdeen-Angus, and Hereford breeds have become available to whoever would enter the field. One has but to choose the breed with which he wishes to work and thereafter follow well-known fundamental procedures. The trail leading toward perfection has been charted, and a considerable body of knowledge, open to anyone, already accumulated. As in all fields of human study, much remains to be learned, but ample available information enables anyone to make an intelligent beginning.

Whatever progress the breeder makes is a benefit to mankind. This of itself lifts him above the sordid level of sheer materialism, selfishness and greed, imparting to him the qualities of the humanitarian. It is a matter of important encouragement for a man to know that, when he has produced a better cow, horse, sheep, or any other creature, he has made as substantial a contribution to human welfare as though he had endowed a hospital or built a library.

Best of all, men who labor in the field are imbued with a spontaneous desire to share their success with others.

I think I should be missing an opportunity if I did not say, from my experience, that a very important addition to the character and qualifications of the men who have entered these agricultural partnerships with me resides in the qualities of their wives and families. From early store days I have found it constructive on all sides to acquaint myself with the nature of the home life of partners. Is it happy? Is the wife of a temperament and willingness to help? As a man seeks to realize his individual ambitions, is his wife one who stands strongly beside him?

When I was personally selecting associates for the company, a man's wife had as much to do in many cases with my choice of him as partner as his qualifications for the job. Without exception wives of the farm managers, notwithstanding multitudinous household tasks, have found time to share in the stockbreeding and related work. Sons and daughters, having come first into harmony with the project through that universal love in children for animals, are now developing talents of their own in relation to developing purebred stock.

It will not seem surprising, therefore, that my agricultural interests have brought me one of the great satisfactions of later life, toning perfectly with the harmony that was touched off in the little chapel at Battle Creek.

In the troublous thirties, when difficulties growing out of the Florida episode were being worked out through the courts, I came face to face with a necessity which I had not imagined could ever touch me and which called, in a curious way, for all the humility I could summon. For three years it was necessary for me to receive again a salary from the J. C. Penney Company. I had drawn salary at Kemmerer from 1902 to 1909. From then until 1932 every dollar I received derived directly and solely from the earnings of my shares in the business of the stores. Since 1935 I have never had a salary.

While I could not ignore the necessity in the circumstances of 1932, in a peculiar way it hurt. Yet it had its constructive side; even though not an easy one to learn, it presented me with a lesson in humility which I knew I must school myself and learn.

When it seemed at times that the job of restoration must surely overwhelm me, my father's words would recur to me. "Jim will make it. . . ."

But I had also to help me an entirely new sense of God's *wanting* me to help myself.

# CHAPTER FOURTEEN

I cannot explain the reason why I did not seek baptism for almost ten years after experiencing the revelation, in the early morning hours at Battle Creek, that God with His abundant love was ever present to help me. Perhaps the sense of release I experienced was but the raising of a curtain, and I needed the discipline, the attunement of thinking, which would make me truly ready to receive God into my life.

It came about in an unexpected and quiet way, which is perhaps the way pervasive change always comes.

One morning in the late thirties I had an engagement to make a talk before a normal school assembly in Chillicothe, Missouri, on the "Application of Christian Principles in Business." I was stopping at the time at my father's old farm, which I now call the Home Place, just outside Hamilton.

I speak quite often on this subject, which seems to me one connected at many points with today's dealings among men. It stems from the principle taught by Christ: "Render unto Caesar the things which are Caesar's, and unto God the things which are God's."

I am a businessman and therefore an amateur at homiletics, so I have some doubt that trained sermonizers would agree that this text is applicable to my theme. Nevertheless, it seems to me that it is a mistake to draw an arbitrary line between the sacred and the secular, and that the measure of man's *whole* duty is the same for business, and service to God. Whether to his business or his God, the man who does not give his best is not doing his whole duty. Success may come in a measure, but unless it is the product of having done one's maximum best, it will be less than it might be, and of a quality to vanish under pressure.

That morning I was particularly anxious to reach these young student teachers with thoughts which might, related to the endeavors into which they would disperse on leaving school, have a constructive effect not only on them but on all with whom they came in business contact. So I said, in part:

"I believe much of the difficulty in the world of business is due to the fact that too many people try to gain materially without giving their best, or are foisting unfair values upon the public.

"When we discuss honesty in the abstract, there is no difference of opinion. It is only when the principle is applied to our activities, particularly our commercial enterprises, that we may contradict one another. No one will say that there is any right of an employee to take a dollar from his employer, or for the head of an organization to increase his prosperity by deceiving the public or underpaying his employees. Yet how often many of us fail not only to give the best goods for the prices asked but also to give our business the best of our minds and talents, the best of our loyalty.

"Success is first of all a matter of the spirit. When I see a young man or young woman identifying him- or herself so closely with the work at hand that the closing hour passes unheeded, I recognize the seeds of success. Young people doing more than is required of them—that is, more than the employer requires—to satisfy the demands of their own consciences are on the way to success.

"My father was a minister and a businessman, both. One of the things about him which made a lasting impression on me was that to him there was no difference between his farm and his church when it came to the faithful performance of duty. He did his best on the farm, in his relations with his fellow-men and in the details of his everyday living; and he was equally consecrated and loyal to his religious service.

"If it is possible to live the Christian life at any point whatever, it should be possible to live it in *all* relationships of one's life. When the individual faces a question of business choice he should ask himself, 'Is this worthy of my best?' If the answer is 'Yes,' he should go into it to the extent not only of upholding his own self-respect, but also of holding fast to the highest Christian standards.

"Some men attain positions of distinction in the business world and are entrusted with responsibilities involving the well-being of hundreds, even thousands, of their fellow-men, while others never get beyond the village store or the country office. Yet again and again I find those who are in positions often regarded as insignificant doing so much for the people of their communities that by comparison those in spectacular positions are shamed.

"Why is this? I believe it is because these little-known people make a habit of giving everything in them to their work, unselfishly counting their gains, not by money profits so much as by the service they are able to render. They do not separate the secular from the sacred but recognize and practice their indivisibility.

"The world at large never heard of my father, yet I know that he was a successful man. He lived largely because he lived truly; he rendered unto Caesar those things that belong to Caesar even as he rendered unto God the things that belong to God.

"We shall not be judged by the Heavenly Father by the material success we achieve, nor yet according only to what we do. We shall be judged by our honesty of purpose, and by the spirit in which we pursue life's duties in all their various phases.

"We should examine carefully our motivating purpose in life. Is it the prospect of material reward, how much we can get by our efforts, to be spent then on our own interests? Or will our purpose be to release fully such powers and talents as we may possess, not only to support our dependents and for our general economic sustenance but also to build a better community, a better state, a better nation, and a better world?

"For my own life program I adopted six principles which I believe contain the essentials of success. Since they have an interrelation with my thoughts on Christian principles in business, I should like to reaffirm them here:

"I believe in *preparation*. Generally we find what we look for; hence our achievement depends largely on our preparation for the business we undertake.

"I believe in *hard work*. Hard work is the only luck a man is justified in counting on; it will mean sacrifice, persistent effort, and dogged determination; never by chance, growth is always the result of a combination of forces.

"I believe in *honesty*. Naturally, the kind of honesty which prevents a man from taking something belonging to someone else. But, too, that finer honesty, which will not allow a man to give less than his best; which makes him count only his hours but his service and opportunities; which constantly urges him to enlarge knowledge and increase efficiency in using it.

"I believe in *reposing confidence in men*. Men who came into the J. C. Penney Company with me have never been put under surety bond. Men who must have halters around their necks to make them do the right thing were not the men for us. I have always preferred letting men know that I rely on them. Those who proved unworthy only caused the others, who far outnumbered them, to stand out. In large measure this principle of reposing confidence in men is responsible for the J. C. Penney Company. Common sense is not thrown away, but we pick good men, then rely on them. So I urge upon you: Believe in yourself, and trust your fellow-men.

"I believe in *appealing to the spirit of men*. One of the wisest men who ever lived said, 'For the letter killeth, but the spirit giveth life.' Every enterprise in which I have been interested demonstrates as a fact that it is the spirit which gives life to character and undertakings.

"I believe in *practical application of the golden rule,* as taught by the Master nearly two thousand years ago. 'Therefore all things whatsoever ye would that men should do to you, do ye even so to them, for this is the law and the prophets.'

"The golden rule is a law of love, underlying all true religion. Observance of the golden rule insures observance of civil law and carries us past the letter of the law to the spirit 'which giveth life.' It makes us willing to sacrifice what is commonly called personal liberty for the welfare of others, willing to forgo indulgences which, however harmless they may seem in our own lives, may work ruin in the lives of others.

"In his *Meaning of Service* Harry Emerson Fosdick says '. . . . to do for others what we desire to have done for us is not a negative ideal. Too often justice is pictured in terms of abstinence from rank injustice. But the golden rule cannot, so negatively, be kept. Justice is positive. It is the painstaking bestowal upon others' lives of the same sort of constant, sacrificial ministry by which we ourselves have lived, without which we could not really live at all.

"'Inherent in most normal human beings is the disposition to defend the weak against the strong. The spirit of the golden rule permeates our ideals of public and private justice, even though the ideals are not always translated into action. Disregard for the golden rule paves the way for untold misery and injustice. As I see it, disregard for the rights and welfare of humanity as a whole, through greed and the lust of conquest by a few minorities, has brought the world to the present terrible impasse.

"'Fear stands in the way of maximum practice of the golden rule, in secular dealings. Many fear that, if they are too generous, they will be unable to meet the competition of their less scrupulous neighbors. They have not comprehended that another principle laid down by the Master is also essential: "Whosoever will save his life shall lose it; and whosoever will love his life for my sake shall find it." '

"Because of the Penney Company's open application of the golden rule in all its relationships,—a radical departure from average policy in the community where the business had its birth,—its early failure was prophesied.

"Yet is is an immutable law that the spirit and practice of service underlie even material success, and service is the principle expressed in the golden rule.

"As a seed must be buried in the cold, damp earth before its blossoms can emerge into the sunlight, so success must be preceded by sacrifice. Self-denial is a basic requirement for accomplishment, whatever the field of endeavor. I know that, not only in theory but from personal experience. No success is easy; it comes out of willingness and following the hard road, the sacrifice of everything but honor to achieve a goal. Diligence in business results in advancement. Unselfishness invites good will, which, in turn, opens opportunities for material progress. Not that I advocate the exercise of un-selfishness with an eye to attaining selfish advantage; I merely wish to point a working of cause and effect.

"My experience has been that employees respond to fair-ness and liberality. A harmony of mind and purpose ensues between employer and employee; the devotion of workers is released, to find expression in ever better work."

I am reminded that a number of men who have been with the company a long time did not find it easy to get in. In some instances a wife has been a factor of doubt as to whether the Penney Company was the right place for a man. I remember at least one instance in which the wife was the one to prove the doubts all wrong.

George Mack, who is at present, our first vice-president

and a director of the company, was an automobile salesman in Everett, Washington. One of his close personal friends was Lew Day, who joined us in 1912 and is another story of determination to associate himself with our philosophy of doing business.

Mr. Mack was satisfied that he could make good with us. But it would involve his beginning at much less money than he was getting, and Lew Day, who interviewed him about joining us, was doubtful. He meant no criticism when he said, "I just don't think Gladys Mack will be able to live on that amount of money."

"I'll show you I'll be able to live on it!" cried Mrs. Mack. And she did, too. We often laughed about the idea that you must never reject a man for a position until you've heard what his wife has to say on the conditions!

I don't have much patience with people I hear saying that it is impossible to get good people for jobs. Won't it follow naturally that if a business idea is basically sound it will draw to itself quality people, not only because of the job but because they want to be connected with business whose underlying idea has vigor, and offers scope for individual initiative? I believe it will, and the history of the Penney Company is filled with illustrations.

In some respects the experiences of Mr. Mack and Mr. Hughes paralleled, in that both were probably earning $3000 to $5000 a year when they quit to come with the Penney Company for $1500 or less, and neither was ever sorry.

Lew Day himself was a case of a man who concerned himself, not with sacrifices, but only with what he considered the opportunities he could find. Selling appealed to him in general, and in particular selling with the Penney Company. Figuratively he trudged many long miles to join us, remaining nearly thirty-five years until his retirement a few years ago.

I recall another man, a schoolteacher in a Utah town, who wanted so much to work for the Penney Company that he offered to work for nothing. Perhaps the manager who interviewed him saw "just a schoolteacher" but for me there is always a special kind of pleasure in seeing a man possessed of a real urge to store selling.

This man was persistent about coming with us, confident that he could and would make good. And he did, first as a salesman, then manager. His case, that of Mr. Hughes, and a number of others, illustrate that schoolteachers who left their profession to come with us made no mistake; they did succeed.

Returning to the suggestions I felt moved to make at that normal school assembley, I said finally:

"Up to the outbreak of the war, business was gradually learning the creative wisdom of applying the golden rule to its dealings with society at large. Increasingly executives of many industries testified to their belief in the practices of this principle, with the result that there was a decided improvement in relations between employer and employees and the number of satisfied customers.

"In international affairs we cannot show the same degree of progress. In the midst of a retrogression to barbarism it often seems that much ground has been lost, as to universal practice of Christian principles. I, for one, believe the ground can be recovered, through rededication to the principle.

"Lest I may be seeming to imply that I have myself made a perfect record of applying Christian principles to all phases of my life, let me say that I had to pass through fiery ordeals before reaching glimmerings of conviction that it is not enough for men to be upright and moral men. When I was brought to humility and the knowledge of dependence on God, sincerely and earnestly seeking God's aid, it was forthcoming, and a light illumined my being. I cannot otherwise describe it than to say that it changed me as a man.

"There was much ground for me to cover and it was to be years before I arrived at a point where I felt ready to affiliate with the church. I must admit it was only after I assumed the responsibility of church membership—thus rendering unto God the things that are God's—that I realized just how merely being a church member, and attending church regularly, is not enough. For all men there must be yet one more thing: giving oneself over to God's purpose.

"I should like to address one word especially to young businessmen. I felt, when our business was started, that the practice of Christian principles, as embodied in the golden rule, was not only desirable but necessary. Yet I must admit that some men succeed who do not follow these principles. Nevertheless, it is my firm conviction that the stepped-up business cycle, with mass production, now profoundly conditioned by the potential of atomic energy, makes their practice an intensely practical necessity. In my early years one might put spiritual things in one compartment of life and business relations in another, and attain a measure of success. Today this is not true in the same way. I therefore take the prerogative of mature experience and urge younger men as they come along to study with great earnestness the relation between Christ's two commandments, to love God, and to love your neighbor as yourselves.

"Working these two great laws into the balance of everyday life there is assurance of a life of spiritual satisfaction and, I believe firmly, one of material prosperity and peace of mind.

"Yet this satisfaction on the spiritual side, and prosperity in the material sense, will ever depend on prayerful search for the right way, *according to God's will*. Self-will and ambition are strongly set in us all. Only continuous prayer and meditation can lead us along the path of service to spiritual satisfaction."

After the normal school assembly a young local minister came up to speak to me. "Mr. Penney," he said, "there is a lot of meat in this talk of yours. I want to ask you to repeat it in my pulpit."

"Oh, I couldn't do that!" I exclaimed impulsively. "I would be out of place. I'm only a businessman—I've never spoken from the pulpit."

But he was an earnest and persuasive young man. Finally, albeit with misgiving, I consented to do what he wished of me.

Sunday morning I drove through bright Missouri spring sunshine the twenty-seven miles to the Chillicothe Christian Church. The young pastor escorted me into the pulpit. I noticed the Lord's Table was spread, an aspect of the service which I had not anticipated. I felt filled with a strange sort of panic and leaned over nervously to speak to the pastor. "I'm afraid this is rather embarrassing," I whispered. "As there is to be a Communion service I must tell you that I have never partaken."

Throughout all the intervening years I had never quite blotted out of my mind the picture of my father and mother, driven from their church on a presumption of heresy. Until the end of his life, every time my father was aware of my bitter thoughts, he counseled me, with grave patience, "Son, they know not what they do. As we forgive, so shall we be forgiven—" Youthful bitterness kept me from church membership for a while; later I found other excuses, many of them more or less related to the comfortable reasoning that, so long as a man made a rule of standing for ethical and moral values, it wasn't absolutely necessary to enter church membership.

The pastor regarded me without dismay. He whispered back, "You're a Christian, aren't you? Well then, there's no reason why you can't partake at the Lord's Table."

Yes, I would say I am a Christian, I thought. Yet, while the pastor busied himself with arranging final markers in hymnbook and Bible, I could not help thinking uncomfortably that not only was I a stranger to the sacrament itself, I was not even familiar with its appointed order.

The pastor rose, gave out the first hymn:

> The King of Love my Shepherd is,
> Whose goodness faileth never. . . .

I found the page, followed the lines.

> Thou spred'st a table in my sight
> Thy unction grace bestoweth. . . .

Suddenly it seemed to me that a voice was speaking quietly to me, saying, "Be not afraid—"

In time and quality the voice could be the voice of my father, who, with my mother, died as strongly in the faith

as he lived. It could be the voice of my mother, who feared
only that she would be less, as a child of God, than she
should be. It could be the voice of One who speaks to us all,
I now believe, at those moments when most we need to hear;
it could be the voice of God.

*Fear not, for I am with thee,* it seemed to say.

Gently the injunction took hold on my mind and heart.
Intangibly I sensed a disentanglement from fear and, slowly,
from prideful embarrassment.

The service neared its climax, in the observance of the
Lord's Supper. The moment had come when I must decide;
for or against, heeding the voice.

In a handful of seconds a feeling came over me, an ineff-
able sense of quietude, of having been helped across a hard
place in a road—

For the first time in my life, that Sunday in Chillicothe,
fear loosed its hold and I partook of Communion.

Throughout the afternoon I thought over the experience
and its meaning to my life. That night I wrote to Mrs.
Penney: "I have come to the point where I want to be baptized and join the church."

As she was a communicant of the Episcopal Church, where
the children were also members, I believed it would be only
natural if she were to prefer that I join that church. But, with
her naturally discriminating taste, she made me understand
that such a decision, being of supreme intimacy, must be left
to the individual.

It chanced that I had recently heard from Dr. Poling the
decisive experience of an old gentleman of eighty-nine, who
had elected to be baptized by immersion because, he said,

"Jesus was immersed, and I wish to be as like Jesus as it is possible for me to be."

I had a thought in connection with being received into the church which was important for me: to be received into the Memorial Church at Penney Farms, such a vitally personal connecting link with my parents' faith and memory.

Here denominational lines were never drawn. Name any Protestant denomination and you were certain to find at least one of its people present. Even so, denominations were not mentioned, simply being checked at the gate, along with titles and learned degrees. It represented, I thought, a wonderful argument for church union; not so much a community, really, as a fellowship, in which the cameraderie of kindred minds could flourish like the roses in the garden, the shrubbery planted around the buildings. These people had come from all points of the country—from corn and wheat country; from rocky Maine, lush California, and the islands of the South Seas, the plains and mountains of Canada, the Kansas prairie. They were missionaries, YMCA and other Christian workers, and preachers, men and women of deep evangelical faith.

This was the church home into which I wanted to be received. Accordingly, Dr. Poling met me at Penney Farms, and I was received into the church there.

The old apprehension, that an action of mine might be misconstrued as a gesture made for effect, was still in the recesses of my mind. I arranged for Dr. Poling to baptize me in a private service.

Mrs. Penney and I journeyed to Philadelphia one Sunday

morning, hearing Dr. Poling preach at the Baptist Temple and afterward lunching at his home. In the early afternoon, assisted by his associate Dr. George Sweet, Dr. Poling conducted the service there.

After brief meditation together there was reading from the Gospel According to St. John, fifteenth chapter: "If ye keep my commandments, ye shall abide in my love; even as I have kept my Father's commandments, and abide in his love."

After a prayer I knelt and was baptized. The whole service was sublimely simple, profoundly moving, and, as I wished, conducted in the presence of only a few of those closest to me.

Pondering it, I felt that it was not that baptism, in itself, had brought about the profound personal change of which I was now clearly aware, but that baptism had been the climactic symbol of the change; grievous experiences and ordeals had worked the change, and the hour of baptism was the crowning moment.

Entering upon a new life, it seemed to me as every day passed that I had never really known the meaning of life at all before. I was greatly struck by the thoughts expressed in Henry Drummond's book *The Greatest Thing in the World*.

"To love abundantly is to live abundantly, and to love forever is to live forever. Hence eternal life is inextricably bound up with love. . . . Eternal life also is to know God, and God is love. This is Christ's own definition. Ponder it. 'This is life eternal, that they might know Thee, the only true God, and Jesus Christ, whom thou hast sent.' Love must be eternal. It is what God is. In the last analysis, then, love is life. . . ."

In the light of this thought, although I believed I had kept the Commandments and dealt ethically with my fellow-men, I had by no means always expressed fully the love of God.

It was my good fortune, in these days when, as you might say, my life was being redesigned and replanned, to make the acquaintance of the Reverend Sam Shoemaker, rector of Calvary Protestant Episcopal Church at Gramercy Park, in New York.

An informal activity of the parish, I found, was a business-men's meeting for prayer and exchange of experiences, at five-thirty after the close of business on Mondays.

On the average twenty or twenty-five men came together. I was invited to join in the meetings and felt buoyed up by contacts with others, businessmen like myself, who were re-cognizing that stubborn self-will, with its pride and compla-cency, would not be overcome—neither would the serenity be forthcoming which God is eager to give us—without a more intelligent and persistent effort on our part to come into, and abide in, God's presence. To this end, we needed to *learn to pray*.

I began to study prayer, as the link to bring man into closer relation with God. I came across a remarkable study of the subject by Dr. Alexis Carrel, the eminent French phy-sician and physiologist, who died in France, it will be remem-bered, in 1944. It made a deep impression on me especially in the light of reputedly insoluble differences of science and religion.

Fifty Years with the Golden Rule     187

This was the essence of Dr. Carrel's analysis of our dilemma:

To us men of the west, reason seems very superior to intuition.
We much prefer intelligence to feeling. Science shines out, while
religion is flickering. We seek first of all to develop intelligence
in ourselves. As to the non-intellectual activities of the spirit,
such as the moral sense, the sense of beauty, *and above all* the
sense of the holy, these are almost completely neglected. The
atrophy of these fundamental activities makes of the modern
man a being spiritually blind. Such an infirmity does not permit
him to be an element good for the constitution of society. . . .
The fact is, the spiritual shows itself just as indispensable to
the success of life as the intellectual and material.

This seems easier to accept as a fact, perhaps, than to translate into actual practice.

There came under my notice too about this time a most
interesting letter written by a Trappist monk to the Laymen's
Movement for a Christian World. In part it went thus:

We Americans want everything in a hurry. Yet an interior life,
dedicated to the practice of prayer, is not the work of a year, or
even ten. We of the high-strung western world seek the natural
outlet of nervous energy in action. It takes us a long time to discover the fact that mental activity can become the best and most
satisfying kind of action, that is the inter-action which takes
place between God and the Praying Soul. . . . There are two main
pitfalls on the road to mastery of the art of prayer. If a person
gets what he asks for, his humility is in danger. If he fails to get
what he asks for, he is apt to lose confidence. Indeed no matter
whether prayer seems to be succeeding or failing, humility and
confidence are two virtues which are absolutely essential.

Another contact developed in this period which was to be
of immeasurable inspiration, a real point of departure for
life as I now wanted to learn to live it. My friend Ralph W.

Gwinn, who was also, as he had been for many years, the J. C. Penney Company lawyer, was closely interested in the Laymen's Movement. One day, as I later learned, in conversation with Weyman Huckabee, executive director of the Laymen's Movement, Mr. Gwinn said, "There's a man who ought to get into working for the Movement. His name is J. C. Penney."

Individual obligation for association in the Movement is, in a sense, simple; that is to say, it can be expressed in twenty-five words:

"As a Christian layman I will try to find my part, and exert my strength, in building Christianity into the everyday life of the world."

In another sense those twenty-five words open vistas of opportunity which are limitless and which, because opportunity is not always easy or convenient, may often demand a bending of will.

Mr. Huckabee and I met first in Mr. Gwinn's law offices, and often subsequently at the Monday meetings at Calvary Church.

When its objectives were outlined to me, active identification with the Laymen's Movement appealed to me as not only an interesting but a challenging prospect.

My dealings throughout my business life had been charted by the compass point of the golden rule; yet for a long time I had had a deep inner longing to better understand the power of God and be used more adequately to give it expression.

I was invited to speak before a Laymen's Movement Conference in Bronxville on the application of Christian principles in business. (I recall that it was in the same year that

I had the honor of being made a 33rd degree Mason, in Washington, D.C.) It was an evening meeting, and by the time the question period was over, I took a train which got me home after one o'clock. Yet as I looked back, the perspective I gained on the question—whether it is possible to be a success in business and at the same time a Christian—would have made it worth while if I had come a thousand miles to be there.

In H. M. Tomlinson's *Gallions Reach* there is a description of the meeting of two men, one of the Occident, one of the Orient. In the Chinese garden surrounding the home of the man of the East, the man from the West notices a wonderful vase of jade. His host remarks, "Come over and take it in your hands; such a vase is made to touch as well as look at." After a moment he adds thoughtfully, "Sometimes I wonder if Western culture changed into chimney smoke because of a neglected sense of touch."

Perhaps we have not related business and being Christians as we might have, through tending to make of spiritual living a jade vase, to look at rather than to touch.

Writing in *Christian Laymen* Mr. Wallace C. Speers has said,

It is the spiritually minded men and women who . . . will in the end be responsible for the creation of a free, democratic world society. We must find a way of coordinating all the spiritual power that exists in the minds and hearts of men and women everywhere of whatever religion or faith, create a new political federation of spiritually minded men and women. . . . Such a federation would cross economic and political boundaries, and be based wholly on the individual's belief in the Supreme Divine Being.

It could become the instrument capable of conditioning political and economic leaders to use their power, in carrying out through political organization the Divine will for a decent, free world, built on mutual respect, mutual faith and mutual responsibility which, in reality, constitute the love which the good Lord said would enable the world to operate successfully.

After the Bronxville meeting Dr. James Fifield of the first Congregational Church of Los Angeles, largest church on the West Coast remarked to me, "Mr. Penney, that is a message which you ought to go out and give all across the country." I had occasionally been in his Los Angeles congregation, and knew his father and mother.

"Oh, I couldn't do that," I said, unconsciously falling back into the sense of inadequacy which would have kept me from the Lord's Table that April Sunday in Chillicothe, Missouri.

But notwithstanding the work Dr. Tapper and I had done in the early years of my being in New York, to the end that I might be more at ease as a public speaker, the idea of speaking to general audiences across the country did not seem for me at all. "I couldn't do it," I assured Dr. Fifield.

In the intervening years I have had abundant reason to be grateful to Dr. Fifield for his rejoinder.

"Oh yes you can," he exclaimed, "if you will only give yourself now, as wholeheartedly as you've given your money in the past."

In that way it came about that I began periodic speaking tours around the country and in Canada for the Laymen's Movement, before large, urban groups and small groups in the kind of little country meeting houses where I went to church and Sunday school as a boy.

It was a help in my studies of the power of prayer to meet

for prayer and silent meditation before breakfast on Friday mornings in Weyman Huckabee's office whenever I was in New York. The discipline of silence increasingly absorbs me.

It can truly be said that every technique of prayer is good which draws man nearer to God, and I believe that sincerely. But I have found a special power in relation to prayer, and that is the element of silence.

To use silence as effectively as do our Quaker friends is perhaps too much to expect of most of us. Yet to learn to be alone with God in the presence of others is something all of us should try to learn. If we will but find them, there are innumerable times during a day when we can turn our thoughts, if only for a moment, from business affairs, to center them on the loving-kindness of God, the love of Christ, and seeking guidance to be of service to our fellow-men.

However necessary our material aid in rehabilitating the stricken world, our responsibility includes obligations of a spiritual nature too. We live in extraordinary times with many hazards ahead. Must we not obligate ourselves to new and ever wider expressions of the Christian ideal?

In the course of time I was privileged also to go as a prayer delegate to sessions of the United Nations at Lake Success.

We all know that there is a continuous need for leaders to work together in a spirit of harmony and unselfishness, that truth and justice may prevail and peace be secured to the world. The idea of prayer delegates is an extension of the Laymen's Movement's having sent Dr. Frank Laubach to Paris in 1946 to organize prayer groups at the Peace Conference to pray daily for the delegates and other world leaders, that they might do God's will for the world.

To be a prayer delegate is simply arranged for. It is a

matter only of obtaining tickets in the ordinary way for such sessions of U.N. meetings as one can attend, and spending the time there in silent prayer that God will guide men in building a better world.

Such experiences fused to put me in a new and invigorating relation to more vital Christian living. Increasingly I discovered that, actually, it was a rather different thing from the casual "living like a Christian" on which I had rather prided myself in earlier years.

More and more I gained perspective, to see how it is that a man may show all external signs of Christian living yet still not attain fullness of life. I began to comprehend that the moral and upright habits, the support of worthy causes with one's means, even joining the church, good as they are in themselves, and commonly associated with the nature of being a Christian, nevertheless do not go far enough. They take for granted that a man is spiritually fully awake, and growing normally in understanding of God's spiritual laws, whereas in reality he well may be only moving along a path of least resistance, in a sort of comfortable twilight sleep.

Where I had for so long instinctively relied on myself, and myself alone, for the power to go forward, *more and more prayer became my main source of strength*. It began to be clearer to me how necessary it is not to forget the need for our actions to conform always to the spirit of prayer. To pray on rising and then for the rest of the day to behave like a pagan is palpably absurd. I realized how much we need really to pray all through the day.

I do not believe one man's method of prayer can, in the

nature of things, be offered as a method for others, for the whole power and use of prayer are too intimate to be translated into technique. One evolves a pattern according to individual hunger for guidance and power. Frankly, a few years ago, if the plan which is now part of my daily living had been proposed to me by someone else, I am pretty sure my reaction would have been, "Fine for you perhaps, As for me—"

As for myself, if it is of any interest and value to others, I keep half a dozen books on a bedside table and always end the day with an interval of meditation and prayer. In this way my last thoughts before going to sleep are on God, on Christ, on my spiritual needs and those of others, to whom, in some way God will direct, I may be of service.

*I am learning to pray, and I feel the efficacy of prayer. In a material sense I have much less now than once I had; but, and I say it most seriously, that no longer seems to matter. What matters is that in place of material possessions I believe I have been guided to a much better conception of what life really means.*

I know now that a full understanding of life is only possible through love of God. Surely we shall come to a more complete love of God through spending some time each day recalling His goodness, our dependence, finally offering returns to Him such as an act of self-denial, an act of kindness to one in need or other trouble, done in His name.

Among the books I keep beside me are the Bible and certain devotional books. Of the latter, one of which I never tire is Drummond's *The Greatest Thing in the World.* Among others things, it has suggested the thought to me that it is not enough to learn *about* spirituality. It seems to me certain that the ills of the world today are bound up in our failure, rather, to have learned, how *to live* spiritually. And surely the primer of such learning is prayer.

It was necessary, too, for me to learn how to give myself over to God's purpose in the full sense. In earlier years, in the company, we gave much time and thought to planning an educational program, with a view to bringing out men's latent talents. Just so, in order to express my faith fully, it has been necessary to find God's purpose for the use of my own latent talents and experience.

On occasion I encounter those who are skeptical that the people one meets in business either know or care whether a man is living the Christian way in his business life. I can only testify from my own experience and observation that people do know, and do care. Many a time during store visitations people who were unknown to me have come up and shaken my hand saying, "We're glad to see a Christian man making a success."

In earlier business periods a businessman could achieve a measure of success by being upright and ethical. Today we know that in many areas of the country the men who are known in the community for positive Christian living are those who lead their communities. On all sides we hear evidence pointing to the prospect that we are on the brink of a great movement of God's spirit. Dr. Elton Trueblood, in his recent book, *Signs of Hope,* takes note of ever increasing groups of young people meeting to pray and positively cultivate the Christian life.

As I became more and more closely associated with the

Laymen's Movement I had frequent occasion to recall what Dr. Short had said, about work which was still ahead for me. It is at once a source of gratification and of regret—regret that many years passed before my mind and heart were opened to the opportunity lying so close at hand; gratification that, through prayer, God's power has been more fully revealed to me, in time to put my "graduate years" to wholehearted and, I hope, useful service, in His name.

## CHAPTER FIFTEEN

"I wish I were a young man again, so I could start all over."
How often we hear that. I have said it myself, and thought it
more times than I have uttered the words.

If I could get a message over to the young people of the
country—indeed, of the world—it would be: *To succeed in
life does not require genius.*

No boy ever worried more about his future and making a
success, or ever left his home town with prospects visibly less
bright, than I. Certainly genius was not one of my qualities.

Any young man or woman of ordinary intelligence, who
is morally sound, open and aboveboard in human dealings,
not afraid of work, prepared to play the game fairly and
squarely and keep everlastingly at it, can succeed in spite of
handicaps and obstacles.

I never feel sorry for poor boys. It is the children of wealth
who deserve sympathy; too often they are starved for incentive to create success for themselves.

I had no material inheritance to give me a start, because
though I can't remember ever going hungry, or being cold
for want of stove fuel, my parents seldom had any cash money
to speak of.

From a worldly standpoint my parents were in humble
position. I was brought up very strictly. My mother flogged

me only once or twice—when we needed such disciplining, for the most part it was our father who took care of it—but on those few occasions the thing which made the impression on me wasn't the flogging itself, which I undoubtedly deserved, but what Mother said to me afterward. I had a very bad temper, which not only got me into a great deal of trouble but gave my mother deep anxiety. After she had punished me she took me into the front room and sat me down on the floor in front of her. She looked at me for a long time and finally said, simply, "Jimmy, a boy can break a mother's heart."

Early I learned to obey, to honor and respect my parents, and to work. When I went out into the world I had the common sense to feel thankful that Christian parents had formed my character. I do not know whether there would be a J. C. Penney Company today if they had not inculcated in me an ineradicable drive to be a good neighbor, and consideration for the rights of others.

When people ask me, "What one factor do you believe has contributed most to the growth and influence of your organization?" I don't have to stop and think about an answer. Unquestionably it has been the emphasis laid from the very beginning upon human relationships—toward the public on the one hand, through careful service, and giving the utmost in values; toward our associates on the other hand.

Were I a young man again, starting all over, it would remain one of my cardinal principles to give men this opportunity to share in what they help to create.

A young man or woman willing to be just a time-server will not succeed. Employees who give no more of their time and interest than sheer necessity demands do not comprehend a vital principle which is as true in business as in the spiritual realm, namely, that a man must "lose his life in order to save it." In other words, he must forget himself in service.

Employees willing to go "so far and no farther" for employers soon complain that they did not "get the breaks." Success—earned success, that is—and real growth never come as the result of chance or "luck." Success is for one who sets a high standard today, a higher one for tomorrow, holding himself gladly to that goal. Nor can employers expect to find in employees standards higher than those they hold for themselves.

My advice to young people today is to let no day pass without pushing personal standards a notch higher.

The law of struggle is the essence of all life—animal, vegetable, and human. Our progress from birth to death is marked by struggle, and rightly so, for when we cease to struggle, dry rot takes over. Young people who count not their hours but their opportunities are the ones who maintain the difficult road to success.

I am reminded of a visit I paid not long since to Joslin's Dry Goods Store in Denver, where I worked for $6.00 a week. In company with the manager of our uptown Denver store and some others, on our way to lunch, I said, as we came to Joslin's, "My first job after leaving home was here; come with me while I stop a moment to see a man I worked with then. He has charge of the basement now."

Not finding the basement manager I spoke to a salesman

who was serving two customers. "Is Johnny Shackleford here?"

"No," he said. "Mr. Shackleford is in the East."

"Well, will you just tell him that J. C. Penney called to pay his respects?"

"Are you J. C. Penney?" the salesman said.

"Yes I am."

"Now think of that," he remarked. "I took your place in this store fifty-two years ago."

Can you imagine my feelings? If I had not set ever higher goals I might still be in Joslin's today—and there would be no J. C. Penney Company.

Who can say that it is *good* for young people to be curbed in the matter of working hours—they who have more ambition than their fellows, whose impulse would be to go back to work nights, not because of being asked to do so but because of interest in the job? If working hours are curbed may not ambition also be curbed, and youth become less interested, less keen?

It is said, "But shorter working hours mean more leisure time."

What will you do with your leisure?

Many a businessman chafes under the demands of his strenuous business, looks forward to the time when he will have sufficient money to retire. When that time comes, the new-found leisure amuses for a while, but a new restlessness soon arises, a disturbing sense of uselessness. It cannot be mere coincidence that men who retire to idleness or superficial recreation after active business careers rarely live many years.

Leisure can become a boon for young people when they are ambitious and of an inquiring mind, for it makes possible the additional education and varied self-improvement which will enable them to do a better job in the vocation.

Yet if I were a young person I believe that, between work and more leisure for education and self-improvement, I would choose work. Work presents no horizons; under our system of free initiative one can go as far as his wishes and qualifications lead.

Nor do I believe, with many, that in facing the so-called cold world of business it is necessary to throw into the discard fundamental principles of honesty, fair dealing, and sobriety in order to succeed.

I completed the work of the lower grades and high school. My father saw to it that I got some practice along the way in handling myself and my concerns. But soon after I left home to make my own way I found myself employed in the store which announced itself frankly as a Golden Rule Store. I had to work hard, to add my share to the store volume. But in doing that I also had to make myself golden rule-minded.

In time the men I worked for established me in my next store as manager, selling me a third interest and putting me entirely on my own responsibility to make the store pay and, moreover, as an acknowledged golden rule store.

I was in a position then similar to that of young people the day after commencement. I had been graduated from the "school" of the parent store, and the time and effort I had invested there were the equipment with which I entered the new world of the store where, instead of being directed by an immediate superior, I had to be my own director, making my own decisions in such a way that not only I but my partners would prosper.

One might deduce that, having arrived at the position of manager, I had become a free agent. Actually I was simply pushed by circumstances and my employers into a new curriculum.

If that seems an odd word to use in relation to storekeeping, let me interpret; in effect my store was a laboratory for intensive, practical operation. Such action demanded constant study and restudy, dictated by two forces: (1) volume to be produced for profit—and to increase volume I had to build my clientele; (2) the golden rule as the compass point, on the one hand, and the principle, on the other, to be kept in operation as the underlying spirit of every transaction.

If I indicate a few of the subjects to which it was necessary for me to "buckle down," young people will understand my reason for believing that success is not for the time-server. In themselves these subjects will not be of any particular interest, but they illustrate the fact that whatever occupation a human being enters he is in an *expandable* position. Life and all its activities may be visualized as a starting point, outward bound and of ever expanding circumference.

I was obliged to study and master manufacture and production of goods as to quality, use, competitive grades, price range, and cost of operation.

My experience is that any occupation must be broken down to its operating details. Successful businessmen in whatever line will counsel you:

"Get a job. Break it down until you have before you a curriculum of essential factors. With all the laboratory technique at your command, study each factor. Commencement exercises, far from being the finish of education, constitute life's most permanent call to action."

To sell a customer helpfully a merchant must know more than the customer does about what he is buying. The merchant operating by the golden rule uses his margin of knowledge to help the customer get more from his purchase, and use what he buys with more efficiency.

In business one learns how to make the most of location and space, the latter for the most effective display. I have seen great changes take place in our store display. I remember beginning to think seriously about appearance in relation to merchandise when I went to work in Evanston. Merchants in those days wanted to impress customers with the size and variety of stock carried, and when I saw goods hanging all over the front of the store, and from lines strung across the ceiling inside, I was shocked, thinking it looked terrible. The effective display of goods always has occupied a good deal of my thought. Eye appeal draws the customer to the store; when he is inside the store it must be maintained, as an incentive to purchasing.

I had learned the importance of location in a rather difficult way, with my store in Kemmerer. Years later people who were there at the time told Dr. Tapper, "We thought Penney was a damned fool, setting up store that way, off the beaten track. But he took care of it by starting right out and giving them such values that pretty soon they didn't care where his store was—just so long as it was there, and open for business."

I had to study my community, its interests, resources, activities, the spread of its trading area. The factor of my cash-and-carry policy was both plus and minus in the development of the store and illustrates the necessity for studying a community and its characteristics.

The mining companies used the coupon system, which meant two things as far as the miners' buying was concerned. They could always buy at the company store, charging purchases against coupons. But when payday came, chances were there would be little pay left for them to receive in hand.

Inasmuch as the miners rarely had much cash money, how, it was asked, could a cash-and-carry store hope to get much of their business?

My answer was, only by such values for the dollar that they couldn't afford *not* to patronize it.

I cannot recollect anything which we did at Kemmerer—or, for that matter, which expresses the governing principles of the J. C. Penney Company—that cannot be applied under existing conditions by today's young people who are determined to succeed. Changes in times have brought some changes in techniques, man training, and technical education; but if one thing has become increasingly clear as the years passed, it is that *the spirit of human service* derives from more than mere technical and mechanical efficiency.

Can we not believe, with John Greenleaf Whittier,

> We give by faith; but faith is not the slave
>     Of Test and Legend. Reason's voice and God's:
> Nature's and Duty's, never are at odds.
>     What asks the Father of His children, save
> Justice, mercy, and humility,
>     A reasonable service of good deeds,
> Reverence and trust, and prayer for light to see,
>     The Master's footprints in our daily ways.

Perhaps we may liken the ideal spirit of service to the *quality* spirit. Quality includes spiritual and intellectual elements; among them are *interest* (you must care about the wants of those who bring you their business) and *service* (you must know that what you furnish in exchange for money will be of maximum usefulness) and *fair dealing* (you must not give in exchange for money anything which you yourself would not consider worth that amount of money, and more).

Failure to give service and value is not only against the spirit of the golden rule but poor economy as well. I am reminded of an instance which made a lasting impression on me back in my home town of Hamilton, when I was a boy, working during summer vacation for a grocer.

I observed that it was a habit of my employer to empty packages of a common coffee into a canister displayed as containing the finest Mocha and Java, selling at nearly double the price of the inferior grade. The grocer had hit on the idea of stretching out his Mocha and Java by selling this mixture at the price of the pure grade.

I told my father about this. It outraged his sense of integrity in business and he took his trade away from the store.

The employee who binds himself to standards of integrity, honesty, and hard work has no need of being supervised; already his supervisor is personal responsibility.

What I have related of my own experiences implies a degree of faith in the active life. No one offered me a soft and easy life, but I do not hesitate to say that the strenuous life was the one which appealed to me, stirring that deeper self which can make it possible eventually to do what may well have seemed impossible. Theodore Roosevelt put it well:

"I wish to preach, not the doctrine of ignoble ease, but *the doctrine of the strenuous life;* the life of toil and effort, of labor and strife; to preach that highest form of success which comes, not to the man who desires more easy peace, but to the man who does not shrink from danger, from hardships, or from bitter toil, but who, out of these, wins the splendid ultimate triumph."

Someone else has said it this way:

"One of the finest thrills in life comes when we get going strong on something we take delight in developing; working it out to a practical result, pushing it a little farther along each day. This may be some enterprise, plan of adventure that combines interest and worthwhileness; the successful issue of which demands that we submit ourselves rigorously to the formative power of Discipline."

To me discipline means, for instance, what Nehemiah did with himself, in rebuilding the walls of Jerusalem. In substance he said, "The Lord directed me. I told no man what He had imparted to me. But I never came down from the wall, or neglected the work."

The application is this: We all work, building and rebuilding, shaping and repairing the walls of that Kingdom on earth which, as the years pass, a Power inspires us to perfect.

When young people complete their main academic education, it is customary to say that they are then passing "into the world of work and responsibility; *life is about to begin*" for them.

Don't believe any such generality!

Believe rather that life long since began for you—began, in fact, when you came into material existence, with a cry at the pain of breath-intake as your first experience. Every day since then you will have testified to your tendency and desires, doing things, showing preferences, defining your character. Thus, so far from having life "about to begin" for you, you are but continuing it in a larger sphere. In many ways you are already what you are going to be. In a measure the pace is set; you have begun to grasp the character of the main road of your travel.

Young people—particularly young men—getting settled in a lifework may have to try their hands at many things, feeling their way along, so to speak. This worries some people, who fear it may indicate instability. I do not feel that way, for there is value in every experience encountered along the way.

A man in one of the leading St. Louis wholesale houses recommended to me a young man named A. F. Lieurance. "He'll make you a good man if only you can keep him from thinking about becoming a dentist," he said; I laughed, because it was a somewhat new competition to me for the services of a man.

Anyhow, I hired him, and he came to work with me in Kemmerer.

But soon he said, frankly "Mr. Penney, I've always had the ambition to be a dentist. I just can't seem to get rid of it. I've decided to go to Kansas City and study."

I hated to see him go. He was one of the best salesmen I'd ever had. I undertook to advise him against leaving.

"Mr. Penney," he said, "I've been taking advice all my life. Now my mind's made up. I'm going to do what *I* think best."

"Well, if that's the way you feel about it," I said, "I guess you have to go." Mr. Lieurance was one of the fifty men who worked with me in the store before Mr. Sams came; if it seems that we must have had a big turnover of help, we did, because nothing but the hardest of hard work would make the store succeed.

Mr. Lieurance did his studying and went to Sapulpa, Oklahoma, where he built up a lucrative practice. But the time came when he must have concluded that there was no great future for him in dentistry, because he applied to Mr. Sams for a job with the Penney Company again. First Mr. Sams put him in Price, Utah, then Murray, where he managed the store. Finally he was sent to California, where he was one of our pioneers, opening the Chico store. He made a great success as a merchant, after getting the dentistry out of his system, and after a while came into the New York office and a place on the Board of Directors. Later he retired, going back to live in California.

When I became a store manager and part owner, everything I had previously done, whether on the farm at home, or in school, or in all the jobs I had held, became of use to me.

Keep this in mind. Within reason, no matter what you may do on the way to your chosen lifework, some day you will find it all turned into capital, for your business investment.

Alert young people map their territory of activity and know it foot by foot. Generally they can be characterized by a few major tendencies; by that, I mean things they do naturally:

They are *skillful* at what they do.

They are *accurate* in their statements.

They are *dependable* in their responsibilities.

Skill, accuracy, and dependability make a firm footing.

Learning to be co-operative can grow from it. All business is done as a result of many minds' turning their energy on a given problem or task. The young person destined for success will not stop at being interested only in his own part of the total job but will study all the contributing aspects which make up operating policy and method. Thus he compares with the symphony orchestra player whose individual instrument is tuned absolutely to the pitch of the whole.

Our first store employed but two people; I was one, my young wife was the other. Today the number of associates in the business that bears my name is approximately 70,000. Consequently I have been privileged to talk with literally thousands of men and women who are associated with us. From all my observations and the evidence produced by these contacts I would say this to young people today:

There is never a day in youth when one should not think most seriously about one's ability and the *best* that can be done with it. It is the nature of ability to pursue a means of expression. Obey its impulse. Shape it to a good end.

One illustration of this which I like to remember is the mutually happy experience of handicapped people and the Penney Company. In 1929, at the time we opened a new warehouse, the Red Cross conferred with us about ways whereby the company could make use of the capacities of handicapped people. As a result, many have found their place with us, doing productive and satisfying work. For instance, one man whose wrist was permanently disabled became a key person in the packing department. A victim of polio, who will be on crutches the remainder of her life, is a most efficient supervisor of a typing division. Another girl who has learned how to live effectively with the limitations of cerebral palsy does well at a certain phase of office work. Another of our associates, who has only one hand, learned to run the mimeograph machine; but he was not satisfied to stop at that. He studied nights to become a mechanical draftsman, and has gone on to make a good foundation in that work.

I had occasion to drop in at the cafeteria in our St. Louis warehouse not long ago. I noticed that all the young people at one table were talking in sign language as they ate lunch. The happiness of their spirits impressed me and when I inquired about them I was told that each one of them was outstanding at his work.

It is a satisfaction to me to know that these are only a few of many handicapped people who are responding to encouragement in the Penney Company to develop their capacities.

The highroad of a lifetime is often a long stretch. If you will be true to the laws of the game, life will fight for you. It will not make the day's work easy. But it will make it possible. It will not block your way maliciously; it may make it hard. But it will make you strong enough to make the grade.

Everything I have experienced since I opened the door of the Golden Rule Store in Kemmerer, Wyoming, that April morning in 1902 only convinces me that, if you have the willingness to play the game honestly and hard, life guarantees you an open road to success.

I have always had implicit faith in the integrity and capacity of the average man, given the proper chance and incentive. I have never asked a man to furnish a surety bond, and everyone who worked with me I have loaded with responsibility just as fast as he could stand it. In my estimation the results show this: Faith not only moves mountains; it builds men.

From my little home town of Hamilton a young man once came to work for me. He had built up a reputation as a first-class failure. Everyone warned me that he would never make good. What was worse, they told *him* so.

Within a year he became very discouraged. I learned about it and wrote him a long letter, telling him how confident I was that he would come through, how disappointed and surprised I would be if he did not.

His store was far up in Idaho, and when my letter reached him it was the dead of winter.

On that same day the mail brought him a letter from someone back in Hamilton telling him that he was a fool and had better give up the job and come home.

"If it hadn't been for your letter, with its note of unbounded confidence, I would have thrown up the sponge then and there," he told me later. As it was, he stayed on, pitching in and working harder than ever. In the end he became one of our most successful men.

Several years ago one of our store managers was doing so poor a job that his case looked hopeless. He came to talk things over with me. After a long talk I still felt certain that deep down in him was the right stuff. Given another chance, I asked, did he think he could make good?

"I know it!" he exclaimed.

So I offered him another store, far from the scene of his failure. The expression on his face told me that he was excited and relieved, but embarrassed too. After a little hesitation he admitted that he didn't even have enough money to move his wife and children to the new post.

I lent him the money to make the move.

In the new environment he made good. Several years later I was having dinner with him and his family in their attractive home and learned that they had made themselves live on spartan fare until they repaid the loan.

I like to think that the main reason men, who had difficulty in striking their stride, wanted very much to stay with me was that they specifically admired a business governed by the everyday practice of the golden rule and wanted to be part of it.

I remember one day in 1913 in Wenatchee, Washington, when the assistant manager of the store there watched all day for a chance to get me in a corner and ask a question. Lew V. Day became our first vice-president in time, and he was never one of those who had serious difficulty in getting under way. He liked our way of doing business, but felt there was so much he had to do to make himself proficient that he said to me, "Is this thing going to last until I have *my* store?"

I have watched hundreds of country boys, cut from a common bolt, making every sacrifice, meeting every emergency to expand under the necessary discipline of early years in business, and climbing to important posts. Hoeing a hard row seems to bring out the best in a man. I remember an incident which brought me in contact with a man who illustrated this truth in a fine way.

A few years ago I was traveling from Denver up to the U.S. Army Remount Station in Nebraska, and when the train laid over for a bit about daylight I went across the street to a little all-night lunchroom for a doughnut and a cup of cocoa.

Someone in the lunchroom must have recognized me and telephoned to the manager of the Penney store in that town. When I was back in the coach the manager came in, looking for me.

"You're Mr. J. C. Penney, aren't you?" he said.

"That's right. Good morning."

"Heard you were passing through and thought I'd get up to come and see you," he said. "You see, I manage the Penney store here. A few years ago I got infantile paralysis—thought I'd never be fit to work again.

"Well sir, the Company treated me so fine, I knew I had to get well, on my feet again, to pay them back. So, Mr. Penney, I bought me a bicycle. It worked out fine—got my legs under me again so I'm almost good as new. This is the first time I ever happened to get the chance to see you, so I thought I'd just come down and meet you." We talked a few moments, and shook hands, and he left.

It pleased me, not as a compliment paid to me, but because of the attitude the Company inspired in him.

As with business, I am convinced that the hard times through which we are passing as a nation hold all the seeds of future flowering. Nothing in life is all of a piece. There's good in bad times, and bad in good times. The swing of business cycles is not just the working of an economic law. I believe it is a method of the Almighty to keep us from growing too soft in prosperity, too sorely tried in the lean years.

The change that has come in my life in recent years convinces me that the universal desire to succeed is a matter which it is entirely proper and necessary to submit to the power of prayer.

Wise men do not argue about the power of prayer. It is a process of mystical relationship with the Higher Being for whom men have many names. As success in business is not merely a matter of opportunity and ability but also the spirit of human service, so also the mystery and power of prayer sustain not only the intellect but the faith of the heart. Success may not come if we pray merely for what we want.

We read in the Gospel According to St. Matthew, "Ask, and it shall be given you; seek, and ye shall find; knock, and it shall be opened unto you." But can we ever succeed at anything unless the true spirit of our supplication is "Thy will be done"?

# CHAPTER SIXTEEN

It was my privilege to deliver the 1949 series of the Green Lectures at Westminster College in Fulton, Missouri. Some observations in those lectures are perhaps worth summarizing since they are pertinent to the purpose of this book.

The John Findley Green Foundation was set up as a framework for expressing Mr. Green's lifelong belief that "the most practical expression of the Christian religion is the improvement of human relationships." There is an affinity between this approach and my own business career, which grew directly out of respect for human relations. From the time I took my first job with Mr. Hale back in my home town I have tried consistently to study how the workaday relations of man to man might be bettered.

In 1937 the Green Foundation established a lectureship at Westminster, with the broad purpose of stimulating interest in and understanding of world problems. The lectures are given annually by men who speak from firsthand experience with economic and social problems of wide concern, suggesting to students attitudes which accord with Christian principles.

I came to the lectureship with a feeling of unworthiness for I was placed in august company. It will be remembered that the term "iron curtain" came into the language by way of the Honorable Winston Churchill's famous speech, delivered in the pleasant brick chapel in 1946. Besides Mr. Churchill my predecessors, of international stature, were Count Sforza, of Italy; Dr. Francis B. Sayre, our former High Commissioner to the Philippines; John Langdon-Davies, of London; Oscar D. Skelton, Dominion of Canada Undersecretary for Foreign Affairs; Dr. T. V. Smith, Professor of Philosophy at the University of Chicago; and Dr. Samuel Guy Inman, Latin-American Affairs lecturer at Yale and the University of Pennsylvania.

Some experiences of my inheritances and merchant life led me to offer the following, among thoughts in the green lectures:

As citizens of One World, in which we have seen poor human relations blight and retard civilization, must we not turn our soberest thinking to a spiritual basis for improving all human relations?

We are prone, I believe, to overlook the significance of the spiritual factor in American destiny and development. It is particularly timely to rethink it now, when we are being misrepresented and otherwise placed in a false light by some whose ideologies are the antithesis of ours, with the intention of weakening faith everywhere in our considered regard for the dignity of man's freedom.

The Christian believer comprehends that things on earth don't just happen but are part of the divine plan.

By destiny and the impact of two world-wide catastrophes America—without motive or volition or, indeed, the psychological wish— has been thrust to the forefront of world power and leadership. Not temperamentally totalitarian-minded, we have yet scarcely had time to orient ourselves in this epoch-making turn of events; some of us are made anxious by it, others are still oblivious to its responsibilities.

Shall we not school ourselves to look on it as evidence of a trust reposed in us by the God of Nations, for the purpose of furthering His benevolent designs?

By what events have American destiny and development been spiritually leavened?

Whatever man's nationalistic ties originally, he is primitively actuated by an irresistible longing for liberty, and hatred for arbitrary government. A prime expression of this truth is the fierce conviction of every human being that he shall be free to worship God as he understands Him.

The foundation of this destiny of ours was in process when a group of people in England, whose austere principles gained for them the label "separatists" emerged as leading opponents of an ancient caste system, rigid land tenures, an established church, and closed political privilege. When their concept of freedom put them at sharp variance with existing laws, customs, tradition, thought, and many of their neighbors and they could bear no more, they emigrated first to Holland, then to Plymouth, Massachusetts. Their spirit and action as Pilgrims were to be forever revered.

In primitive, untouched surroundings they made their brave new beginning. Civil shackles left behind, their church their own, with an efficiency which became a model for others they set up for themselves a government the like of which had never been seen. In form and working it was a true democracy, founded on the fundamental proposition that it is the nature of men to be free—free in religion, in work, in speech, in civil and political action—within the limits of laws framed for the protection of all.

It is significant that instinctively they called upon God for help in establishing laws which were right and just.

Common denominators exist between those days and our own. The establishing and maintenance of freedom demands moral discipline and unselfish vision.

The innovation of a society rooted in religion and liberty presented hardships and setbacks but no natural incompatibility. Containing a constructive contagion, it soon gathered others to its example. The Dutch, who built New York; the Quakers and Irish, who migrated to Pennsylvania, the Swedes of Delaware; the English Catholics of Maryland; the English who colonized Virginia, North and South Carolina, and Georgia; the French Huguenots of South Carolina; the Spanish settlers in California and New Mexico, the French and Spanish of Louisiana—after one form or another, all professed the Christian faith, making it the basis for their settlements. It set the pattern for the stamp of spiritual aspect on all our ensuing national growth.

The spiritual wellsprings of our life and creative power are our homes and our churches. Long before we are aware of it, the home makes an ineradicable impression upon us. When we arrived on earth we took our place in a group of people who inevitably began to reproduce in us their very selves, through their thoughts, ideals, standards of conduct, and religious faith. This process was foreordained by the Benign Creator in constituting the family as the microcosm of human living. Thus, in the finest sense, provision was made for each of us to be the product of the moral, intellectual, and spiritual ideals of the home in which we were reared. In the home which nurtured us we received our first revelation of human relations.

Happy are those born of Christian parents and reared in Christian homes! Throughout the years of my adult life I have had uncounted reasons to be grateful that I was such a one. My Old School Baptist minister-father labored unendingly to teach his children by precept and example what he preached from the pulpit on the Sabbath—that a Christian home is a wellspring of spiritual living and power. My mother's similar conviction found living expression in the manner of home she made for us.

It was not easy for her by any means. Educated in the convent, brought up in well-to-do surroundings with no occasion to turn her hand to any work, when she married and went to Missouri with her young husband she lived in the pioneering way of his hardy forebears who possessed the wealth of courage and determination but no material substance whatever.

Pioneering is a fire burning out dross, refining the gold of character, and only the sturdy of soul come through. I have never ceased to marvel at the courage, fortitude and spiritual confidence of my parents. The backbreaking, heartbreaking toil, the ceaseless grind from early morning till late at night, the leanness of times and the bereavements were enough to tear down the stoutest fiber. Life in such conditions would have been crushing indeed without a living faith in God, the steady glow of love, the sanctification of sacrifice for the sake of the coming generation, whose bulwark for future success and useful happiness must be a home rich in Christian faith and strength.

From our spiritual wellsprings come our capacities for unselfishness. Our earliest acquaintance with the beauty of unselfishness usually comes in very simple, and thereby long-lasting terms.

I well remember a neighbor's giving me a stick of candy, and my taking it home to show my mother. She divided it among us, but put her share on the shelf. "I will save that for the children," she said. It filled me with a sense of wonder. To us sweets were great and rare treasures, and to see her deny herself made me wish to have some of her goodness.

When I became old enough to see my father and mother as they were, and to appreciate them more nearly as they deserved, I asked myself, "What has made them as they are?" In time I grasped the reason.

*It was their simple and direct faith in God and their sincere love for Jesus Christ, His Son.* This was the wellspring of their beauty of character, pure ideals, inexhaustible courage, and abiding trust and peace. Had I been reared in any other environment my life would surely have been very different. Therefore my deep conviction is based on intimate experience, that the highest duty of parents is to build Christian homes, in whose influence children can grow spiritually strong.

One of the starting points for our world role today is more homes where Christ is honored and the Law of God is regarded as supreme. By a wise exercise of His authority God decreed that the family should be the primary medium through which knowledge of Himself and His wisdom could be transmitted from generation to generation. "And these words, which I command thee this day, shall be in thy heart; and thou shalt teach them diligently to thy children, and shalt talk of them when thou sittest down in thine house, and when thou walkest by the way, and when thou liest down, and when thou risest up. And thou shalt bind them for a sign upon thine hand, and they shall be as frontlets between thine eyes. And thou shalt write them upon the posts of thy house, and on thy gates." Thus were directions given to parents to Israel, that they should give strict personal attention to the religious education of their children in the home.

"Thou shalt teach them diligently . . . ," that is, again and again; "when thou sittest down in thine house . . . ," meaning in the family circle, making the truth of God a topic for congenial everyday conversation; "when thou walkest by the way . . . ," referring no doubt to using illustrations from Nature, to impress upon youthful minds the power and glory of God; "when thou liest down, and . . . risest up . . . ," not losing any opportunity, however slight, to turn the mind toward Eternal Truth; "for a sign . . . and . . . frontlets . . . ," referring to the writing of important words upon bits of parchment and binding them to the wrists or foreheads of children as a reminder of the Word of God, very common among the ancient Hebrews; "And thou shalt write them upon the posts of thy house, and on thy gates" to remind all who passed that those dwelling within were servants of the Most High.

In some quarters it is considered old-fashioned or naïve to

plead for better Christian homes. I never apologize for doing so because my entire business experience tells me that successful dealings between men, in business, government, and social relationships, are influenced for good or ill by home backgrounds. Christian homes are more important even than government because government of the individual in relation to the common good begins in the home. Christian homes were the seed plot in which the unique principles of our country germinated and bore fruit. The hope of their continuance lies as the same source. Our nation, as it has been from the beginning and now is, cannot fulfill its destiny without the vitalizing force of the Christian home.

For proof need we look further than at the history of once proud Germany? For a thousand years the land of the Teutons, regardless of political variations, was a center of Christian culture. It gave the world some of the greatest Bible scholars who ever lived, and the German Christian home was famed throughout the civilized world.

The tragedy of World War I intervened, and later the even blacker tragedy of Adolf Hitler's Nazi order. Churches were abandoned, the Christian home was destroyed, Christian virtues were crucified. The transformation from what Germany was once to a stronghold of a monstrous Nazi Antichrist was so sweeping that few people under thirty years of age can comprehend a Germany which ever was anything other than what World War II revealed her to be.

The companion wellspring of the home, as an influence on human relationships, is the church. Honesty compels me to confess humbly that, although I never lost my belief in the church, and made a point of attending worship with con-

siderable regularity, for a long time I did not fully and freely
unite myself before my fellow-men with the church. Friends
of mine in the ministry discussed with me with great patience
the dynamic differences between a genuine religious experience and even the most faithful adherence to an uncompromising standard of ethical human dealings. But considerable time was to be lost while I was not confronted with the
impact of desperately needing God in my life, and I was not
properly receptive to their anxiety for my fuller spiritual
experience. I evaded the issue by telling myself I was unworthy to unite with the church; what was still worse, I remained indifferent for a long time to the obligation of
seeking God's help in making myself worthy. Through the
experience God has given me, as a result of letting Him into
my life I have learned how badly I cheated myself by not
putting myself much earlier completely in His hands. As He
directs, I am trying to use the powers developed in me by life
in His service.

Is not our great task through the church to which we are
related to confront the world with the Christian ideal in
action?

Within the span of my lifetime sweeping changes in everyday living have occurred in the world. I have seen the advent
of the telephone, automobile, radio, movies, high-speed
roads, the airplane, and—what is surely the most crucial in the
sense of what use we make of it—the discovery of atomic
energy. Life has lost many of the harsh aspects it presented to
my youth. Whole areas of daily living have been completely
altered, and the end is by no means in sight; rather are we on
the threshold of even more marvelous changes. Yet, while

much of what lies upon the surface of our living has changed, man remains *man*, what he was in the beginning, a fusion of God-given potentialities.

In a sense, that fact clarifies our responsibility. Not only do the fundamental nature and needs of humankind remain what they have always been. Behind the church lies almost twenty centuries of divinely planned experience in ministering to them. Church history is a proved source of inspiration and instruction, showing clearly the progressive achievement of God's purpose in the world. The anguished cry of Job, "Oh that I knew where I might find Him, that I might come even to His seat!" expresses the universal longing of mankind. Through the centuries the church has recognized the longing and labored faithfully to satisfy it.

Notwithstanding cynical judgments, its labors have not been in vain. Countless millions the world round have been strengthened to bear with burdens, comforted in sorrow, endowed with nobility of soul for action, through having found God in the ministry of the church.

With his need for God, man needs power also to attain the Christian ideal. What is the Christian ideal? I know no better expression of it than the apostle Paul's brief yet beautiful summary, in his letter to the church at Philippi: "Finally, brethren, whatsoever things are true, whatsoever things are honest, whatsoever things are just, whatsoever things are pure, whatsoever things are lovely, whatsoever things are of good report; if there be any virtue, and if there be any praise, think on these things." This is an enunciation of the Christian ideal of service, clarified further by Christ's statement concerning the purpose of His own life: "The Son of man came not to be served, but to serve, and to give his life as ransom for many."

Following the precept of Christ, the church has always taught that the natural, inevitable expression of the genuinely Christian life is *devoted service,* and working hard at it.

We need to work harder at it now than ever before. Only in that way can the "new" world for which we all pray be created. In a sense there is nothing new about this. Always the church has urged men toward ever and ever higher levels of living and service; only there can they meet the gentle Nazarene, who said, "I am come that they might have life, and have it more abundantly."

It is encouraging that when men have attained some degree of the Christian ideal of service, and begun to move on the higher levels, one of the first results is that their relations with their fellows are improved.

By relating ourselves dynamically with the church we can bring the influence of the Gospel to bear on all human relations. Christ had in mind that faith in God and direct use of Christian principles enlightens men, in whatever phase of living, when He said, "Follow me."

There is no question that Jesus envisioned a world different from that of His day and—may we ponder it deeply— different in many important ways from the world of our day.

That beautiful new world, which hitherto had existed only in the hopes and longings of the race, was inaugurated by Him, and carried forward by a handful of those changed by His example from what they had been when He found them. When their days were done, their unfinished task passed on to others. Today the task, still unfinished, has come into our hands.

Doubtless at no period in history have there been so many plans and ideas as now for remodeling the world. All are not agreed as to those plans and ideas, but all are agreed on the essential need—*the world must be changed.* And many are agreed on the *Christian plan,* which presupposes that men changed by Jesus Christ will use their new power to life the standard of social, economic, and political institutions of the world in which men must continue to live.

I have in mind a representative of certain American business interests who made a survey of European conditions, for the purpose of recommending ways and means to strengthen and stabilize economic life on that continent. He made a careful study of the standardization of currency, river and canal navigation, railroad transportion, and customs duties and bases for imports and exports. He returned with the considered judgment that any suggested programs would have to revolve around the root cause of social, economic, and political chaos, namely, a deep-seated spiritual sickness. "If we would economically stabilize Europe," he said, "first we must minister to Europe's spiritual decline." This diagnosis is timeless; men who are spiritually sick can never be well in the other ways.

The hope which carries us along, as followers of Christ, is the imperishable truth that He can heal the spiritual sickness of men. I do not say this as a theologian but as a plain man who has himself experienced the change worked by God in human beings.

*I believe that to strengthen the home and church as well-springs of spiritual life and power on a national and world scale each of us must renew and rededicate his faith in God.*

What is that faith? I like the definition given in the Book of Hebrews: "Now faith is the assurance of things hoped for, the conviction of things not seen." The hopes of the man of faith are so real, tangible, that he is able to function as though they were already materialized. Faith is the power to make the invisible visible, to bring God down into the common, intimate affairs of life, to set the spiritual above the temporal in relation to them, to adjust ourselves by that compass to the present moment.

You and I need faith to believe that a world changed will ultimately triumph, made new by those spiritual forces which center in the home and church. I say *ultimately*. It could be that the crowning hour in which God looks upon His finished work, finding it good, is far in the dim future. When we recall, for instance, that it was approximately two thousand years from the days of Abraham to the birth of Christ, we comprehend time, sometimes reckoned in milleniums, as necessary to the working out of His plans.

But what of that, if our faith is *the assurance* of things hoped for? If so be that we view the promised land from afar, let us rejoice that it does lie yonder indeed; that in due time those who come after us will enter into it.

It seems certain that we are on the threshold of new tests, an interlude of new tribulation. Contradictory signs—spiritual deterioration dueling with evidences of zeal and consecration to the Christian way of life—are everywhere.

Which way will *we* tip the balance in our time?

In other lands the church and the disciples of our Lord

have in the last thirty years passed through fiery furnaces of affliction. Vigorous, unrelenting efforts have been made to snuff out the light. They have not succeeded. In the ultimate sense they never will. But the price paid to keep the glow even feebly alive has in some instances been all but crushing.

While we in this country still enjoy our traditional liberties it is well for us to remember prayerfully that today more than half a billion people live on this earth in spiritual thralldom, directly or indirectly under the absolute control of inexorable totalitarian forces, one of whose fundamental aims is the complete destruction of free democracy and faith in God wherever they have flowered on the face of the earth.

If this calamity is averted it will be by the upsurge of mighty faith in God. Wherein lies any other hope?

The apostle Paul, knowing that a long, hard struggle confronted the early Christians, again and again used the expression, "Stand firm in the faith!" He urged them to be watchful, strong, and courageous. When we add another figure of speech, which he addressed to young Timothy, his characterization of the Christian as a warrior is complete: "Fight the good fight of faith!" Firmness, aggressiveness for a spiritual basis of living, must be our watchwords today. Sounds of battle are in the air. Each of the faithful is challanged to stand his ground and fight.

> My soul, be on thy guard;
> Ten thousand foes arise;
> The hosts of sin are pressing hard
> To draw thee from the skies. . . .

As churchmen this is our task. Though huge, it is, I believe a hopeful one and, while the present circumstances should stir our most prayerful concern, there is no warrant for despair.

In his letter to the church at Ephesus the apostle Paul urged Christians to don the breastplate of righteousness, shoes of the gospel of peace, the shield of faith, the helmet of salvation, and the sword of the spirit. Most important, in order that the man in his armor might be truly invincible, he urged him to "pray always with all prayer and supplication in the spirit."

If our homes and churches are to be spiritual wellsprings, sustaining the truth in purity to improve human relations with all men everywhere, we must begin on our knees. As a man to whom the power of prayer is doubly precious for having discovered its full efficacy only in recent years, I am convinced that, in the good fight to faith, too little prayer contributes more certainly to defeat than too little fighting.

Receiving our criteria in the home and the church, how can we translate them into the action of our human relationships, to the good of the world?

All my life the golden rule has been to me the great instrument for this purpose. From experience I can testify that it will work when given the opportunity.

As guides for thought and action, ethical principles never change. They stand like lofty mountain peaks. Hidden today by the clouds of our own insufficiency, illumined tomorrow by the brilliant sunshine of God's strengthening, seen and unseen they are always there, an eternal, unchanging part of earthly environment.

Fundamental ethical principles, as expressed in the Ten Commandments, have been at the disposal of mankind since the dawn of Christian Civilization, changing not so much as a hair's breadth. Time and history have not affected them for they are immutable, like unto Him who said, "I am the Lord, I change not."

I do not say that the golden rule is easy to follow in business or any other human relationships. I say that it is not easy. It does not adapt itself to divided allegiance. The man proposing to chart his life by the golden rule will experience the truth immediately that a man cannot serve two masters. The perfect exemplar is Jesus, with his total obedience to the Way. It was not by accident or coincidence that, when He delivered to the twelve the incomparable discourse which Christendom cherishes as the Sermon on the Mount, much of it dealt with principles governing human relations, and that the climax of His subject was reached when He said, "So, whatsoever ye would that men should do to you, do ye even so to them." He did not hold out the prospect to them that it would be easy, but He made them know it was humanly possible.

*To follow it genuinely, in spirit and deed, would usher in the golden age indeed, transforming the tragedy-ridden world into a garden of matchless peace.*

My initial acquaintance with the golden rule, though I did not then fully comprehend it as such, was in the tutelage of my father.

My first experience with a business institution which undertook to do business by the golden rule, frankly advertising the fact, came when I had left home and gone to work in the store in Longmont. The fact that the proprietors not only knew how to organize and conduct a drygoods store but could operate it profitably by the golden-rule method inspired me, particularly because I grew to young manhood hearing cynical people say that it is impossible to be a success in any form of commercial activity and still abide by Christian principles of living.

Having inherited the persuasion to be both an honest Christian and a successful businessman, I wanted to believe that the gulf between a man's ethical and moral standards and his everyday self-interest was imaginary, and that I could apply Christian principles in business life and succeed.

In Longmont I had the authorization of my employers to practice the golden rule with every customer I served. Each passing day only impressed me more, that in actual practice it did work.

When I went to Kemmerer as third partner in my first independent venture, I was committed publicly as an individual to do business in accordance with the golden rule. I had no doubt of making good on that basis. It meant simply treating my working associates and customers as I would be willing to have them treat me in a human relationship.

The cynical refer to the love of money as the root of all evil. My first year's experience at Kemmerer taught me instead that the function of money is that of a tool to be kept busy, by conversion into goods people need and will buy. As money came across our counters in exchange for goods at a fair profit, it went out again immediately for more goods, which people needed to be able to buy at fair prices.

There was a major need for really trained men who would comprehend the principle of this cycle and keep it in motion.

Finally I resigned as President of the company to devote my time to discovering and training men with the qualities to become executives of the future. Within four months of opening a personnel office in St. Louis we received approximately five thousand applications, sixty-three of which were accepted and the applicants employed.

Our plan was not solely to make money, but also to develop men by training. If we trained men effectively, profits would take care of themselves.

No person should be employed in any business institution to be left as he was when the institution found him. It is impossible to induce better service and enthusiasm from the dead-level ability of a fixed, unchanging person. Change is vital, improvement the logical form of change. Our training was designed explicitly to enlarge self-respect, deepen self-confidence, multiply efficiency, and prepare men for the wider responsibility which alone can broaden and enrich lives.

No matter what his position or experience in life, there is in everyone more latent than developed ability; far more unused than used power.

I have always believed an expression of the golden rule is to assist development of men's latent abilities, to unleash unused powers. I am happy to recognize that many businessmen and executives concur in this view. More and more men of broad vision and sensitive spirit are coming around to believe that the most important element in business is human relations, that the principal factor in human relations is spiritual. This leads many of us to the prayerful hope that the day is dawning when a business institution will be visualized, not in terms of assets, inventories, and profits, but as a group of individuals, joined by mutual interest, working harmoniously toward a common goal for the conservation of human good.

Business never was and never will be anything more or less than people serving other people. People who sell serve those who buy, and vice versa. In the J. C. Penney Company from the beginning we have visualized customers as our neighbors, whom it is our neighborly privilege to assist toward buying what they need and want at the lowest fair prices. We respect their rights and wishes. Saving money for our customers we effect for ourselves economies in operation, goods are guaranteed as represented, worthless merchandise is never stocked, and a homelike and congenial atmosphere is created within our doors, carrying out into the community to speak for us.

In other words, we interpret the golden rule as the *mandate of service*. Applied to business or social relations, domestic, national, or international, the principle of service is the same. It is human nature for people to be responsive to any attempt to render them genuine service.

The dilemma of the world today cries out for a finer, deeper sense of service than has yet been known. Businessmen are in a privileged position to brighten conditions and lighten burdens under which mankind gropes today.

I do not believe that there is any basic resistance to applying spiritual principles to human relationships. There is fear, but I do not believe inherent selfish unwillingness. Many people strive to shed their fear, feeling, with the Psalmist, "Behold, how good it is for brethren to dwell together in unity." All of us sense the need for a higher moral and spiritual code in every phase of human living, and yearn to find the way to do our part.

We sense also that we cannot set ourselves at rights with one another, solve our vexing problems, or move out effectively into a new area of national greatness unless we enshrine God at the center of things.

Shall we not keep reminding ourselves that, wherever the Gospel of Jesus, and Christianity, have been honored, a way has appeared out of critical circumstances, seemingly insoluble problems, and hopeless confusions?

Here, then, is the clarion call for the application of the golden rule in our inclusive relationships. After utilizing the golden rule in the long years of my business as instinctively as I use twine to tie a parcel, I simply give it as my conviction that no other rule known to the mind of man is sufficient to solve our problems and develop future good.

In the golden rule the twin laws of justice and love are met. Said the prophet Micah, "He hath showed thee, O man, what is good; and what doth the Lord require of thee, but to do justly, and to love mercy, and to walk humbly with thy God?" Said Paul the apostle, whose majestic intellect was dedicated to comprehending the personality, mission and message of Jesus, "Let love be without dissimulation. Be kindly affectioned one to another, with brotherly love; in honor preferring one another. . . . Love suffereth long, and is kind; love envieth not; love vaunteth not itself, . . . doth not behave itself unseemly, seeketh not her own, is not easily provoked, thinketh no evil; . . . . beareth all things, believeth all things, hopeth all things, endureth all things. . . . And now abideth faith, hope, love, these three; but the greatest of these is love."

We need not ask ourselves whether, if we apply it to our everyday relationships, the golden rule will fail to carry us to success. Shall we not ask, rather, "Will I fail the golden rule?"

In this critical day shall we not renew our relationships to home and church and to God, freely giving Him control of our hearts to govern us, in order that we may discharge our responsibilities as individuals of His creation in the improving of all human relations?

These thoughts drawn from the lectures I delivered at Westminister College epitomize most sincere personal beliefs. I have introduced them into this book in the hope of their serving a further purpose.

# CHAPTER SEVENTEEN

I remember an incident in one of the stores a few years ago. I was in an important conference with the manager and some of the men when someone came into say that a customer was demanding to see me personally. They had told him that I was on limited time and very busy, but he said he'd come a long way for the purpose of seeing me, and intended to do so. He said something else about a paper of needles, which they couldn't altogether understand.

I went out to greet the man. "I'm Mr. Penney," I said. "Did you want to see me?" He was a tall, raw-boned country man, a proud man, who looked you straight in the eye.

"Yes I did," he said. "Wife wants a packet of needles. Been trading in your store a long time, but I never saw you. Heard you was in town. Made up my mind I'd just buy the packet o' needles from you."

I got the needles from the shelf and we chatted a moment. I noticed the overalls he was wearing weren't our Payday brand, which I believe are the finest overalls made. I sold him a pair of those, and some other things, in fact quite a bill of goods. It gave me a chance to discuss the golden rule way of doing business, how and why our Company has made a point of it from the beginning.

When he left I thought perhaps he had insisted on my waiting on him our of curiosity, to find out if there was such a
man as J. C. Penney. But then I thought that perhaps he had
been interested only in seeing a personification of the Company, rather than some one man. Either way it gave me a
pleasant feeling to take back to the meeting, and a reminder
of my responsibility to the public, reflected in that man as a
customer.

I gained insight too into the responsibilities laid upon
what I might call the "institutionalized man" when I was
visiting in the Los Angeles area. At the home of Ingle Barr,
who formerly was in our real-estate department, I happened
to remark that I have yet to take my first cocktail.

"Don't do it, Mr. Penney," Mr. Barr said; "there are so
many of your friends and associates who would be disappointed."

Times come to everyone, unless we are just clods, when we
try to stand apart from ourselves and see that person whom
others see in us. Emerson said, "An institution is the length-
ened shadow of one man." And yet no man can be himself
alone; he is the sum of all the influences of all his associations. I am not inclined to think of the Penney Company as
a creation of mine. It is bigger than anything I could ever
create or be. It is the finest example I know of co-operative
effort; men sharing in what they helped to create have made
it what it was. Whatever I had to do with its beginning, by
injecting a few cardinal ideas into the selling of merchandise,
has come back to me a hundred-fold in the confidence—and I
think I may say, humbly, the love—of my associates. All along

the way they have strengthened me with their esteem; the desire to be worthy of them has made me a better man.

Christianity is a set of principles governing human conduct, a conditioning power by which, if we will let Him, God can make our abilities more adequate in the service of mankind.

My reason for joining the other businessmen who are active in the Laymen's Movement for a Christian World was that its purpose all the time is to find more ways of building Christianity into the everyday life of the world.

All of us need to keep constantly before us the intimate relation between Christ's all-important commandments: to love God, and to love our neighbors as ourselves. A balanced expression of these two great laws in our everyday lives will constantly open opportunity to serve our fellow-men and bring to ourselves deeper spiritual satisfaction.

The "graduate years" of our lives are good; they afford us time and the leisure to review the Source whence cometh our help, and the chance to pass along some of the blessings bestowed upon us.

In this connection I am reminded of two meetings, rather different in character, yet illustrating the privilege of service to our fellow-men. As I have already said, I once received sustaining comfort from a chance visit to a rescue mission in New York, at a time of intense grief and confusion. For that reason I have always felt a deep responsibility to such institutions, and the wish to be used by God to help other distressed souls, as I was helped.

One night a year or two ago I dropped in at one of the city missions. The men gathered there were singing a hymn which was a favorite of my mother's, "My faith looks up to thee." Near by I noticed a man who was plainly much affected by the hymn. He was in sorry condition. I sensed that he knew it all too well, and felt it the more acutely because of some intimate association which the hymn had brought to mind.

Quietly I moved over to him. "That was one of my mother's favorites," I said. "I can see her, going about her housework in the kitchen of our farm home back in Hamilton, Missouri, and humming that melody. Did your own mother happen to be fond of it?"

The eye he turned to me were soul-sick. With difficulty to get the words out he mumbled, "My mother used to sing in church—the choir—I can hear them—'My faith looks up to thee'—"

"Wherever she is, son, she still has faith in you." I said.

The music went on:

> While life's dark maze I tread,
> And griefs around me spread
> Be Thou my guide.
> Bid darkness turn to day,
> Wipe sorrow's tears away,
> Nor let me ever stray,
> From Thee aside. . . .

I said, "My friend, why don't you come back now to God? I'm sure you knew Him once—"

But he was hunched over in his seat, and seemed so lost in misery that I doubted if he even took in what I was saying.

After a moment I said, "If I go with you, will you go forward?" I understood so well the ways in which we hold back. . . . I could recall my own experience back in Chillicothe, ridding myself of self-fear, making up my mind to partake of Communion.

He looked up at me with a kind of exhausted relief, almost eagerness. Part of his misery, I thought, had been that he desperately wanted to break away, go back to God for help, and that he couldn't seem to make himself take the first step. "Yes, I will," he whispered.

Thereby, for the first time in my experience, God gave me the privilege of leading a fellow-man to His altar. He had indeed blessed me, if I could have even the smallest part in helping one person. Experience has taught me that the faith in God which we need cannot work in us through casual acceptance of a standard of moral conduct but that we must stand close to Him, looking for guidance and strength in all things, through constant prayer.

The other meeting I have in mind was a privileged one too, not long before he passed away, with Paul P. Harris, founder of Rotary International, who, with his wife Jean, lived for thirty-seven years in a woodland home "on the only hill in Chicago."

I had felt drawn to Rotary because of the similarity between its underlying principles—"Service above self" and "He profits most who serves best"—and the motto of the J. C. Penney Company, which is Honor, Confidence, Service and Cooperation.

I have always made a point of 100 per cent attendance at Rotary, and have been the gainer by it. The visit with Paul

Harris seemed to crown the stimulation of trying to be truly a Rotarian.

I understand it was one of his dearest desires to have his home on a hill. Shut off from the drive by towering old oaks, surrounded by a variety of beautiful wild fruit trees, and constantly enlivened by the caroling of all manner of birds, the Harris home eloquently expressed the spirit of its occupants and their dedication to the meaning of Rotary.

Over a cup of tea that afternoon we exchanged experiences with the founding of institutions on sound principles, and the visit made an impression on me which I shall never forget.

As I come to the close of this informal account of some personal experiences along the road to deeper spiritual sensibility I want to convey some thoughts bearing on faith in God, and the future.

Recent national and world events have not shaken my faith in the ultimate triumph of freedom and justice. My parents ingrained in me their faith in God, and belief that *right* always triumphs eventually. Today my faith is not shaken, and I do not doubt the final victory of *right*.

I do, however, emphasize the words *ultimate,* and *final,* for I believe we may have to pass through a period of great trial. It seems to me that we are living in prophetic days; for a time *evil* may hold sway, even appearing to override *good*. I am reminded here of the minister who said that, if we knew our Bible, we would not need to read newspapers!

But I believe we must accept these conditions, and possibly even greater tribulations, as part of the world's destiny, without losing our faith that in due time right will triumph over might. We cannot believe otherwise so long as we believe in the existence, in the justice, and in the holiness of God.

A store manager wrote me recently that these are times which tend to fill everyone with pessimism. That should not be so. We should recognize the times for what they are—times of tribulation, but not for giving up. Rather should such experiences inspire us to re-examine our faiths and re-establish our convictions more firmly, resolving to acquit ourselves like men with faith so deep and abiding that it cannot be shaken by external events.

Thinking along this line I am strongly reminded of the life of Earl C. Sams, which has drawn to the close of its earthly phase as this book is being finished. It was a shock to us, for it came suddenly, but many things in our experience with the man himself temper the blow.

Mr. Sams' life was characteristically devoted to casting his lot with ideas he could believe in. He came to Kemmerer to work with me in 1907 for the reason that he believed the idea of the Golden Rule Store was right and, because it was, offered him the opportunity for which he was looking.

He combined with an unlimited capacity for hard work an unusual—I might say almost uncanny—judgment. Perhaps his greatest gift was his ability to put himself in the other person's place. He understood people and their human problems instinctively. As a consequence, everyone who came in contact with him felt his warmth and, at the same time, his humility.

Whatever he touched succeeded, for he entered into every job with his heart, and all of his heart. Customers had confidence in him, and no greater thing can be said of any merchant. Throughout his lifetime he studied to improve his service to his fellow-men. In 1917 he took my place as President of the company and in that position his hand was sure. In 1946 he became Chairman of the Board. He was recognized as one of the leaders of business in our time.

Mr. Sams was himself a happy man, and he would not want us to mourn him. Nor do we, rather giving thanks for his life. At funeral services for him there was no need to argue the Christian faith, because the life we met to remember was its own argument for its triumphal going on. I can hear Earl Sams saying, as he so often did, "Keep up the good work!"

As long as we have faith in God at all, we must know that He is all-powerful, that His will for the world is justice and right, and that His purpose will eventually be established here on earth.

Good often emerges slowly, but we must never doubt its final victory.

These are my convictions as to the world aspect in its relation to an overruling Providence.

As to our country, my faith in our America, in its people, and in the "American way of life" is unwavering. Its founding I believe to have been divinely ordained, and God has a mighty mission for it among the nations of the world. It was founded in prayer, in faith, and in the heroic spirit of sacrifice. Lives of comparative ease might have been the lot of our forefathers in their own country had they been willing to surrender their convictions. They chose the *hard right*, rather than the *easy wrong*, and were ready to lay down their lives for freedom to worship God according to the dictates of their own consciences. We know they underwent grievous hardships; many did lay down their lives; and throughout the nation's history, when the occasion has made necessary, their descendants have paid the supreme sacrifice upon battlefields, to preserve these principles of freedom.

Lincoln spoke well: "It is rather for us to be here dedicated to the great task remaining before us. . . that this nation, under God, shall have a new birth of freedom—and that government of the people, by the people, for the people, shall not perish from the earth."

Our country could have been mightier than it is had not some throughout every period of its history retarded its growth by greed, corruption in high places, petty partisanship in crucial periods, and individual selfishness. Selfishness, of course, is the festering spot in every evil situation, whether world, nation, or individual.

As a nation, and as individuals, our fate will always be determined by our choice of the *hard right* or the *easy wrong*. Softened by comfortable living in easygoing periods, our spiritual and our physical muscles tend to become flabby. We need reversions to difficulties to toughen us up. Periods such as the present are testing times. The harder they become, the more determined we should be not to be swept aside by the fears and doubts that bedevil the world.

We must return to the right principles in our thinking, in our beliefs, and in our practices, putting aside negativeness and self-indulgence. No matter what lies ahead we must carry on to the best of our ability, doing our utmost *from day to day,* each in his own niche. In such times those who are too soft, who lack the courage and stamina to strive, slacken effort. Real men tighten their belts, throw full weight into the harness of their daily activities, and pull with all their might and main.

It seems to me that anyone inclined to question whether one can be a business success and a good Christian at one and the same time need look for reassurances no further than to the words spoken by the Lord to Joshua, when He bade him lead the children of Israel across the river Jordan into the land which was to be their home: "This book . . . shall not depart out of thy mouth; but thou shalt meditate therein day and night, that thou mayest observe to do according to all that is written therein: for then thou shalt make thy way prosperous, and then shalt have good success."

To young people setting out on their life's work, to those with most of their adult years ahead of them, and to those casting about for useful, satisfying service to do in their "graduate years" I commend this thought for meditation:

Christ's injunctions, to "Love God," and to "Love thy neighbor as thyself," are practical keystones for the edifice of living. Worked out in everyday life through human relationships, they will provide a balance yielding fruitful service and spiritual blessing.

I once heard this question posed to a minister of the Gospel. "What do you consider the most important words in Scripture?"

He replied without hesitation. "Mark 5:36. 'Be not afraid, only believe.' "

Every aspect of world condition today opens a way provocatively for applying Christian principles to living.

Let us not be afraid; loving God, and our neighbors as

ourselves, let us only believe. Being not afraid, and believing, let us choose for ourselves the *hard right*. If individuals in sufficient number will pledge their part as men willing to follow the hard right, our America will be made safe for her own people and will stand as a beacon light of hope to this war-torn, war-weary world.

My life has passed through a number of phases. Looking back at the ups and downs, the disappointments and the satisfactions, the decade which I believe was the most important to me of all was the second one of my existence. That was the period in which the lasting impression by an unselfish and saintly mother and a good and dedicated father was made on me. If I had not received their early training, and the inspiration of their example to deal with others as I would be dealt with, and to do as good a job as my powers allowed, there would be no Penney Company today and I might never have entered into that joy and peace of mind which comes with the certain knowledge of the everyday and everlasting love and power of Jesus Christ our Lord.